THE TRAGEDY OF JULIUS CÆSAR

THE TRAGEDY OF JULIUS CÆSAR

BY

WILLIAM SHAKESPEARE

ILLUSTRATED BY VARIOUS ARTISTS

CBY STUDENT EDITION

CBY PUBLISHING 2016

MIDDLESEX

TABLE OF CONTENTS

THE TRAGEDIE OF
IVLIVS CÆSAR.

Actus Primus. Scœna Prima.

Enter Flauius, Murellus, and certaine Commoners ouer the Stage.

Flauius.

HEnce: home you idle Creatures, get you home:
Is this a Holiday? What, know you not
(Being Mechanicall) you ought not walke
Vpon a labouring day, without the figne
Of your Profeffion? Speake, what Trade art thou?

Car. Why Sir, a Carpenter.

Mur. Where is thy Leather Apron, and thy Rule?
What doft thou with thy beft Apparrell on?
You fir, what Trade are you?

Cobl. Truely Sir, in refpect of a fine Workman, I am
but as you would fay, a Cobler.

Mur. But what Trade art thou? Anfwer me directly.

Cob. A Trade Sir, that I hope I may vfe, with a fafe
Confcience, which is indeed Sir, a Mender of bad foules.

Fla. What Trade thou knaue? Thou naughty knaue,
what Trade?

Cobl. Nay I befeech you Sir, be not out with me: yet
if you be out Sir, I can mend you.

Mur. What mean'ft thou by that? Mend mee, thou
fawcy Fellow?

Cob. Why fir, Cobble you.

Fla. Thou art a Cobler, art thou?

Cob. Truly fir, all that I liue by, is with the Aule: I
meddle with no Tradefmans matters, nor womens matters; but withall I am indeed Sir, a Surgeon to old fhooes:
when they are in great danger, I recouer them. As proper men as euer trod vpon Neats Leather, haue gone vpon my handy worke.

Fla. But wherefore art not in thy Shop to day?
Why do'ft thou leade thefe men about the ftreets?

Cob. Truly fir, to weare out their fhooes, to get my
felfe into more worke. But indeede fir, we make Huly-
day to fee Cefar, and to reioyce in his Triumph.

Mur. Wherefore reioyce?
What Conqueft brings he home?
What Tributaries follow him to Rome,
To grace in Captiue bonds his Chariot Wheeles?
You Blockes, you ftones, you worfe then fenfleffe things:
O you hard hearts, you cruell men of Rome,
Knew you not Pompey many a time and oft?
Haue you climb'd vp to Walles and Battlements,
To Towres and Windowes? Yea, to Chimney tops,
Your Infants in your Armes, and there haue fate
The liue-long day, with patient expectation,

To fee great Pompey paffe the ftreets of Rome:
And when you faw his Chariot but appeare,
Haue you not made an Vniuerfall fhout,
That Tyber trembled vnderneath her bankes
To heare the replication of your founds,
Made in her Concaue Shores?
And do you now put on your beft attyre?
And do you now cull out a Holyday?
And do you now ftrew Flowers in his way,
That comes in Triumph ouer Pompeyes blood?
Be gone,
Runne to your houfes, fall vpon your knees,
Pray to the Gods to intermit the plague
That needs muft light on this Ingratitude.

Fla. Go, go, good Countrymen, and for this fault
Affemble all the poore men of your fort;
Draw them to Tyber bankes, and weepe your teares
Into the Channell, till the loweft ftreame
Do kiffe the moft exalted Shores of all.

Exeunt all the Commoners.

See where their bafeft mettle be not mou'd,
They vanifh tongue-tyed in their guiltineffe:
Go you downe that way towards the Capitoll,
This way will I: Difrobe the Images,
If you do finde them deckt with Ceremonies.

Mur. May we do fo?
You know it is the Feaft of Luperrall.

Fla. It is no matter, let no Images
Be hung with Cefars Trophees: Ile about,
And driue away the Vulgar from the ftreets;
So do you too, where you perceiue them thicke.
Thefe growing Feathers, pluckt from Cefars wing,
Will make him flye an ordinary pitch,
Who elfe would foare aboue the view of men,
And keepe vs all in feruile fearefulneffe. *Exeunt*

*Enter Cefar, Antony for the Courfe, Calphurnia, Portia, De-
cius, Cicero, Brutus, Caffius, Caska, a Soothfayer: after them Murellus and Flauius.*

Cef. Calphurnia.

Cask. Peace ho, Cefar fpeakes.

Cef. Calphurnia.

Calp. Heere my Lord.

Cef. Stand you directly in Antonio's way,
When he doth run his courfe. Antonio.

Ant. Cefar, my Lord.

Cef. Forget not in your fpeed Antonio,
To touch Calphurnia: for our Elders fay,

k k The

ACT I.

> great feast held in caesar's honour.

SCENE I. *ROME. A STREET*

Enter FLAVIUS, MARULLUS, *and certain* Commoners *over the stage*

FLAVIUS. Hence! home, you idle creatures, get you home:
Is this a holiday? what! know you not,
Being mechanical, you ought not walk
Upon a labouring day without the sign
Of your profession? Speak, what trade art thou?

CARPENTER. Why, sir, a carpenter.

MARULLUS. Where is thy leather apron and thy rule?
What dost thou with thy best apparel on?
You, sir, what trade are you?

COBBLER. Truly, sir, in respect of a fine workman, I am but, as you would say, a cobbler.

MARULLUS. But what trade art thou? answer me directly.

COBBLER. A trade, sir, that I hope I may use with a safe conscience; which is, indeed, sir, a mender of bad soles.

FLAVIUS. What trade, thou knave? thou naughty knave, what trade?

COBBLER. Nay, I beseech you, sir, be not out with me: yet, if you be out, sir, I can mend you.

MARULLUS. What mean'st thou by that? mend me, thou saucy fellow?

COBBLER. Why, sir, cobble you.

FLAVIUS. Thou art a cobbler, art thou?

COBBLER. Truly, sir, all that I live by is with the awl: I meddle with no tradesman's matters, nor women's matters, but withal I am, indeed, sir, a surgeon to old shoes; when they are in great danger, I recover them. As proper men as ever trod upon neat's-leather have gone upon my handiwork.
FLAVIUS. But wherefore art not in thy shop to-day?
Why dost thou lead these men about the streets?

COBBLER. Truly, sir, to wear out their shoes, to get myself into more work. But, indeed, sir, we make holiday, to see Cæsar and to rejoice in his triumph.

MARULLUS. Wherefore rejoice? What conquest brings he home?
What tributaries follow him to Rome,
To grace in captive bonds his chariot-wheels?
You blocks, you stones, you worse than senseless things!
O you hard hearts, you cruel men of Rome,
Knew you not Pompey? Many a time and oft
Have you climb'd up to walls and battlements,
To towers and windows, yea, to chimney-tops,
Your infants in your arms, and there have sat
The live-long day, with patient expectation,
To see great Pompey pass the streets of Rome:
And when you saw his chariot but appear,

The citizens of Rome wanted Pompey to be their leader, not Caesar, wants to see him walking the streets.

~ 10 ~

Have you not made an universal shout,
That Tiber trembled underneath her banks
To hear the replication of your sounds
Made in her[28] concave shores?
And do you now put on your best attire?
And do you now cull out a holiday?
And do you now strew flowers in his way
That comes in triumph over Pompey's blood?
Be gone!
Run to your houses, fall upon your knees,
Pray to the gods to intermit the plague
That needs must light on this ingratitude.

FLAVIUS. Go, go, good countrymen, and, for this fault,
Assemble all the poor men of your sort;
Draw them to Tiber banks, and weep your tears
Into the channel, till the lowest stream
Do kiss the most exalted shores of all.

[*Exeunt all the Commoners*]

See, where their basest metal be not mov'd!
They vanish tongue-tied in their guiltiness.
Go you down that way towards the Capitol;
This way will I: disrobe the images,
If you do find them deck'd with ceremonies.

MARULLUS. May we do so?
You know it is the feast of Lupercal.

FLAVIUS. It is no matter; let no images
Be hung with Cæsar's trophies. I'll about,
And drive away the vulgar from the streets:
So do you too, where you perceive them thick.

These growing feathers pluck'd from Cæsar's wing
Will make him fly an ordinary pitch,
Who else would soar above the view of men,
And keep us all in servile fearfulness.

[*Exeunt*]

SCENE II. *A PUBLIC PLACE*

Enter CÆSAR; ANTONY, *for the course;* CALPURNIA, PORTIA, DECIUS, CICERO, BRUTUS, CASSIUS, *and* CASCA; *a great crowd following, among them a* Soothsayer.

CÆSAR. Calpurnia!

CASCA.
                    Peace, ho! Cæsar speaks.
CÆSAR.
                                Calpurnia!

CALPURNIA. Here, my lord.

CÆSAR. Stand you directly in Antonius' way,
When he doth run his course. Antonius!

ANTONY. Cæsar, my lord?

CÆSAR. Forget not, in your speed, Antonius,
To touch Calpurnia; for our elders say,
The barren, touched in this holy chase,
Shake off their sterile curse.

ANTONY.
                    I shall remember:
When Cæsar says 'Do this,' it is perform'd.

[Handwritten top note: Caesar turns down the crown three times!]

CÆSAR. Set on; and leave no ceremony out.

[*Flourish*]

SOOTHSAYER. Cæsar!

CÆSAR. Ha! who calls?

CASCA. Bid every noise be still. Peace yet again!

CÆSAR. Who is it in the press that calls on me?
I hear a tongue, shriller than all the music,
Cry 'Cæsar!' Speak; Cæsar is turn'd to hear.

SOOTHSAYER. Beware the Ides of March.

CÆSAR.
                    What man is that?

BRUTUS. A soothsayer bids you beware the Ides of March.

CÆSAR. Set him before me; let me see his face.
CASSIUS. Fellow, come from the throng; look upon Cæsar.

CÆSAR. What say'st thou to me now? speak once again.

SOOTHSAYER. Beware the Ides of March.

CÆSAR. He is a dreamer; let us leave him. Pass.

[*Sennet. Exeunt all but* BRUTUS *and* CASSIUS]

CASSIUS. Will you go see the order of the course?

[Handwritten margin note: soothsayer warning caesar about ides of march (15th march – Deadline for settling debts). He is dismissed as a dreamer. Shakespear has reduced the time between the events. Lupercalia was held on the 15th feb; here it is the day before the ides of march, (15th march)]

~ 13 ~

BRUTUS. Not I.

CASSIUS. I pray you, do.

BRUTUS. I am not gamesome: I do lack some part
Of that quick spirit that is in Antony.
Let me not hinder, Cassius, your desires;
I'll leave you.

CASSIUS. Brutus, I do observe you now of late:
I have not from your eyes that gentleness
And show of love as I was wont to have:
You bear too stubborn and too strange a hand
Over your friend that loves you.

BRUTUS.
                                    Cassius,
Be not deceiv'd: if I have veil'd my look,
I turn the trouble of my countenance
Merely upon myself. Vexed I am
Of late with passions of some difference,
Conceptions only proper to myself,
Which give some soil, perhaps, to my behaviours;
But let not therefore my good friends be griev'd —
Among which number, Cassius, be you one —
Nor construe any further my neglect,
Than that poor Brutus, with himself at war,
Forgets the shows of love to other men.

CASSIUS. Then, Brutus, I have much mistook your passion;
By means whereof this breast of mine hath buried
Thoughts of great value, worthy cogitations.
Tell me, good Brutus, can you see your face?

BRUTUS. No, Cassius; for the eye sees not itself
But by reflection, by some other things .

CASSIUS. 'Tis just:
And it is very much lamented, Brutus,
That you have no such mirrors as will turn
Your hidden worthiness into your eye,
That you might see your shadow. I have heard,
Where many of the best respect in Rome,
Except immortal Cæsar, speaking of Brutus,
And groaning underneath this age's yoke,
Have wish'd that noble Brutus had his eyes.

BRUTUS. Into what dangers would you lead me, Cassius,
That you would have me seek into myself
For that which is not in me?

CASSIUS. Therefore, good Brutus, be prepar'd to hear:
And, since you know you cannot see yourself
So well as by reflection, I, your glass,
Will modestly discover to yourself
That of yourself which you yet know not of.
And be not jealous on me, gentle Brutus:
Were I a common laughter , or did use
To stale with ordinary oaths my love
To every new protester; if you know
That I do fawn on men and hug them hard,
And after scandal them; or if you know
That I profess myself in banqueting
To all the rout, then hold me dangerous.

[*Flourish and shout*]

Cassius is being smarmy, he clearly wants Brutus to join the conspiracy, he doesn't directly ask, just suggests that one people are persistant for Brutus to lead Rome.

BRUTUS. What means this shouting? I do fear, the people
Choose Cæsar for their king.

CASSIUS.

                          Ay, do you fear it?
Then must I think you would not have it so.

BRUTUS. I would not, Cassius; yet I love him well.
But wherefore do you hold me here so long?
What is it that you would impart to me?
If it be aught toward the general good,
Set honour in one eye and death i' the other,
And I will look on both indifferently;
For let the gods so speed me as I love
The name of honour more than I fear death.

CASSIUS. I know that virtue to be in you, Brutus,
As well as I do know your outward favour.
Well, honour is the subject of my story.
I cannot tell what you and other men
Think of this life; but, for my single self,
I had as lief not be as live to be
In awe of such a thing as I myself.
I was born free as Cæsar; so were you:
We both have fed as well; and we can both
Endure the winter's cold as well as he:
For once, upon a raw and gusty day,
The troubled Tiber chafing with her shores,
Cæsar said to me, 'Dar'st thou, Cassius, now
Leap in with me into this angry flood,
And swim to yonder point?' Upon the word,
Accoutred as I was, I plunged in,
And bade him follow: so indeed he did.
The torrent roar'd, and we did buffet it

With lusty sinews, throwing it aside
And stemming it with hearts of controversy;
But ere we could arrive the point propos'd,
Cæsar cried, 'Help me, Cassius, or I sink!'
I, as Æneas, our great ancestor,
Did from the flames of Troy upon his shoulder
The old Anchises bear, so from the waves of Tiber
Did I the tired Cæsar: and this man
Is now become a god, and Cassius is
A wretched creature, and must bend his body
If Cæsar carelessly but nod on him.
He had a fever when he was in Spain;
And, when the fit was on him, I did mark
How he did shake: 't is true, this god did shake:
His coward lips did from their colour fly;
And that same eye whose bend doth awe the world
Did lose his lustre. I did hear him groan:
Ay, and that tongue of his, that bade the Romans
Mark him and write his speeches in their books,
Alas, it cried, 'Give me some drink, Titinius,'
As a sick girl. Ye gods, it doth amaze me
A man of such a feeble temper should
So get the start of the majestic world
And bear the palm alone.

[*Shout. Flourish*]

BRUTUS. Another general shout!
I do believe that these applauses are
For some new honours that are heap'd on Cæsar.

CASSIUS. Why, man, he doth bestride the narrow world
Like a Colossus, and we petty men
Walk under his huge legs, and peep about

To find ourselves dishonourable graves.
Men at some time are masters of their fates:
The fault, dear Brutus, is not in our stars,
But in ourselves, that we are underlings.
Brutus and Cæsar: what should be in that 'Cæsar?'
Why should that name be sounded more than yours?
Write them together, yours is as fair a name;
Sound them, it doth become the mouth as well;
Weigh them, it is as heavy; conjure with 'em,
'Brutus' will start a spirit as soon as 'Cæsar.'
Now, in the names of all the gods at once,
Upon what meat doth this our Cæsar feed,
That he is grown so great? Age, thou art sham'd!
Rome, thou hast lost the breed of noble bloods!
When went there by an age, since the great flood,
But it was fam'd with more than with one man?
When could they say, till now, that talk'd of Rome,
That her wide walks encompass'd but one man?
Now is it Rome indeed, and room enough,
When there is in it but one only man.
O, you and I have heard our fathers say
There was a Brutus once that would have brook'd
Th' eternal devil to keep his state in Rome
As easily as a king.

BRUTUS. That you do love me, I am nothing jealous;
What you would work me to, I have some aim:
How I have thought of this and of these times,
I shall recount hereafter; for this present,
I would not, so with love I might entreat you,
Be any further mov'd. What you have said
I will consider; what you have to say
I will with patience hear, and find a time
Both meet to hear and answer such high things.

Till then, my noble friend, chew upon this:
Brutus had rather be a villager
Than to repute himself a son of Rome
Under these hard conditions as this time
Is like to lay upon us.

CASSIUS. I am glad that my weak words
Have struck but thus much show of fire from Brutus.

Enter CÆSAR *and his train*

BRUTUS. The games are done, and Cæsar is returning.

CASSIUS. As they pass by, pluck Casca by the sleeve;
And he will, after his sour fashion, tell you
What hath proceeded worthy note to-day.

BRUTUS. I will do so. But, look you, Cassius,
The angry spot doth glow on Cæsar's brow,
And all the rest look like a chidden train:
Calpurnia's cheek is pale; and Cicero
Looks with such ferret and such fiery eyes
As we have seen him in the Capitol,
Being cross'd in conference by some senators.

CASSIUS. Casca will tell us what the matter is.

CÆSAR. Antonius!

ANTONY. Cæsar?

CÆSAR. Let me have men about me that are fat,
Sleek-headed men, and such as sleep o' nights:

Yond Cassius has a lean and hungry look;
He thinks too much: such men are dangerous.
ANTONY. Fear him not, Cæsar; he's not dangerous;
He is a noble Roman, and well given.

CÆSAR. Would he were fatter! but I fear him not:
Yet if my name were liable to fear,
I do not know the man I should avoid
So soon as that spare Cassius. He reads much;
He is a great observer, and he looks
Quite through the deeds of men: he loves no plays,
As thou dost, Antony; he hears no music:
Seldom he smiles, and smiles in such a sort
As if he mock'd himself, and scorn'd his spirit
That could be mov'd to smile at any thing.
Such men as he be never at heart's ease
Whiles they behold a greater than themselves,
And therefore are they very dangerous.
I rather tell thee what is to be fear'd
Than what I fear, for always I am Cæsar.
Come on my right hand, for this ear is deaf,
And tell me truly what thou think'st of him.

[*Sennet. Exeunt* CÆSAR *and all his train but* CASCA]

CASCA. You pull'd me by the cloak; would you speak with me?

BRUTUS. Ay, Casca; tell us what hath chanc'd to-day,
That Cæsar looks so sad.

CASCA. Why, you were with him, were you not?

BRUTUS. I should not then ask Casca what had chanc'd.

CASCA. Why, there was a crown offer'd him; and being offer'd him, he put it by with the back of his hand, thus; and then the people fell a-shouting.

BRUTUS. What was the second noise for?

CASCA. Why, for that too.

CASSIUS. They shouted thrice: what was the last cry for?

CASCA. Why, for that too.

BRUTUS. Was the crown offer'd him thrice?

CASCA. Ay, marry, was't, and he put it by thrice, every time gentler than other; and at every putting by mine honest neighbours shouted.

CASSIUS. Who offer'd him the crown?

CASCA. Why, Antony.

BRUTUS. Tell us the manner of it, gentle Casca.

CASCA. I can as well be hang'd as tell the manner of it: it was mere foolery; I did not mark it. I saw Mark Antony offer him a crown—yet 'twas not a crown neither, 'twas one of these coronets—and, as I told you, he put it by once: but, for all that, to my thinking, he would fain have had it. Then he offer'd it to him again; then he put it by again: but, to my thinking, he was very loth to lay his fingers off it. And then he offer'd it the third time; he put it the third time by: and, still, as he refus'd it, the rabblement hooted and clapp'd their chopp'd hands, and threw up their sweaty nightcaps and utter'd such a deal of stinking breath because Cæsar refus'd the crown, that it had almost chok'd Cæsar; for he swounded and fell down at it: and for mine own part, I durst not laugh, for fear of opening my lips and receiving the bad air.

CASSIUS. But, soft! I pray you: what, did Cæsar swound?

CASCA. He fell down in the market-place, and foam'd at mouth, and was speechless.

BRUTUS. 'Tis very like; he hath the falling-sickness.

CASSIUS. No, Cæsar hath it not; but you, and I,
And honest Casca, we have the falling-sickness.

CASCA. I know not what you mean by that, but I am sure Cæsar fell down. If the tag-rag people did not clap him and hiss him, according as he pleas'd and displeas'd them, as they use to do the players in the theatre, I am no true man.

BRUTUS. What said he when he came unto himself?

CASCA. Marry, before he fell down, when he perceiv'd the common herd was glad he refus'd the crown, he pluck'd me ope his doublet and offer'd them his throat to cut. And I had been a man of any occupation, if I would not have taken him at a word, I would I might go to hell among the rogues. And so he fell. When he came to himself again, he said, if he had done or said any thing amiss, he desir'd their worships to think it was his infirmity. Three or four wenches, where I stood, cried, 'Alas, good soul!' and forgave him with all their hearts. But there's no heed to be taken of them: if Cæsar had stabb'd their mothers, they would have done no less.

BRUTUS. And after that, he came, thus sad, away?

CASCA. Ay.

CASSIUS. Did Cicero say any thing?

CASCA. Ay, he spoke Greek.

CASSIUS. To what effect?

CASCA. Nay, and I tell you that, I'll ne'er look you i' the face again: but those that understood him smil'd at one another and shook their heads; but, for mine own part, it was Greek to me. I could tell you more news too: Marullus and Flavius, for pulling scarfs off Cæsar's images, are put to silence. Fare you well. There was more foolery yet, if I could remember it.

CASSIUS. Will you sup with me to-night, Casca?

CASCA. No, I am promis'd forth.

CASSIUS. Will you dine with me to-morrow?

CASCA. Ay, if I be alive, and your mind hold, and your dinner worth the eating.

CASSIUS. Good; I will expect you.

CASCA. Do so: farewell, both.

[*Exit*]

BRUTUS. What a blunt fellow is this grown to be!
He was quick mettle when he went to school.
CASSIUS. So is he now, in execution
Of any bold or noble enterprise,
However he puts on this tardy form.
This rudeness is a sauce to his good wit,
Which gives men stomach to digest his words
With better appetite.

BRUTUS. And so it is. For this time I will leave you:
To-morrow, if you please to speak with me,
I will come home to you; or, if you will,
Come home to me, and I will wait for you.

CASSIUS. I will do so: till then, think of the world.

Well, Brutus, thou art noble; yet, I see,
Thy honourable metal may be wrought
From that it is dispos'd: therefore it is meet
That noble minds keep ever with their likes;
For who so firm that cannot be seduc'd?
Cæsar doth bear me hard, but he loves Brutus:
If I were Brutus now and he were Cassius,
He should not humour me. I will this night,
In several hands, in at his windows throw,
As if they came from several citizens,
Writings, all tending to the great opinion
That Rome holds of his name; wherein obscurely
Cæsar's ambition shall be glanced at:
And after this let Cæsar seat him sure;
For we will shake him, or worse days endure.

[*Exit*]

SCENE III. *THE SAME. A STREET*

Thunder and lightning. Enter, from opposite sides, CASCA, *with his
sword drawn, and* CICERO

CICERO. Good even, Casca: brought you Cæsar home?
Why are you breathless? and why stare you so?

CASCA. Are you not mov'd, when all the sway of earth
Shakes like a thing unfirm? O Cicero,
I have seen tempests, when the scolding winds
Have riv'd the knotty oaks, and I have seen
Th' ambitious ocean swell and rage and foam,
To be exalted with the threatening clouds;

But never till to-night, never till now,
Did I go through a tempest dropping fire.
Either there is a civil strife in heaven,
Or else the world, too saucy with the gods,
Incenses them to send destruction .

CICERO. Why, saw you any thing more wonderful?
CASCA. A common slave — you know him well by sight —
Held up his left hand, which did flame and burn
Like twenty torches join'd, and yet his hand,
Not sensible of fire, remain'd unscorch'd.
Besides — I ha' not since put up my sword —
Against the Capitol I met a lion,
Who glaz'd upon me and went surly by
Without annoying me: and there were drawn
Upon a heap a hundred ghastly women,
Transformed with their fear, who swore they saw
Men all in fire walk up and down the streets.
And yesterday the bird of night did sit
Even at noon-day upon the market-place,
Hooting and shrieking. When these prodigies
Do so conjointly meet, let not men say,
'These are their reasons; they are natural;'
For, I believe, they are portentous things
Unto the climate that they point upon.

CICERO. Indeed, it is a strange-disposed time:
But men may construe things after their fashion,
Clean from the purpose of the things themselves.
Comes Cæsar to the Capitol to-morrow?

CASCA. He doth; for he did bid Antonius
Send word to you he would be there to-morrow.

CICERO. Good night then, Casca: this disturbed sky
Is not to walk in.

CASCA.
                    Farewell, Cicero.

                                        [*Exit* CICERO]

                    Enter CASSIUS

CASSIUS. Who's there?

CASCA.
                    A Roman.

CASSIUS.
                    Casca, by your voice.

CASCA. Your ear is good. Cassius, what night is this !

CASSIUS. A very pleasing night to honest men.
CASCA. Who ever knew the heavens menace so?

CASSIUS. Those that have known the earth so full of faults.
For my part, I have walk'd about the streets,
Submitting me unto the perilous night,
And thus unbraced, Casca, as you see,
Have bar'd my bosom to the thunder-stone:
And when the cross blue lightning seem'd to open
The breast of heaven, I did present myself
Even in the aim and very flash of it.

CASCA. But wherefore did you so much tempt the heavens?
It is the part of men to fear and tremble

When the most mighty gods by tokens send
Such dreadful heralds to astonish us.

CASSIUS. You are dull, Casca; and those sparks of life
That should be in a Roman you do want,
Or else you use not. You look pale and gaze
And put on fear and cast yourself in wonder,
To see the strange impatience of the heavens:
But if you would consider the true cause
Why all these fires, why all these gliding ghosts,
Why birds and beasts from quality and kind,
Why old men, fools, and children calculate;
Why all these things change from their ordinance,
Their natures and preformed faculties,
To monstrous quality, why, you shall find
That heaven hath infus'd them with these spirits,
To make them instruments of fear and warning
Unto some monstrous state.
Now could I, Casca, name to thee a man
Most like this dreadful night,
That thunders, lightens, opens graves, and roars
As doth the lion in the Capitol,
A man no mightier than thyself or me
In personal action, yet prodigious grown,

And fearful, as these strange eruptions are.

CASCA. 'Tis Cæsar that you mean, is it not, Cassius?

CASSIUS. Let it be who it is; for Romans now
Have thews and limbs like to their ancestors;
But, woe the while! our fathers' minds are dead,
And we are govern'd with our mothers' spirits;
Our yoke and sufferance show us womanish.

CASCA. Indeed, they say the senators to-morrow
Mean to establish Cæsar as a king;
And he shall wear his crown by sea and land,
In every place save here in Italy.

CASSIUS. I know where I will wear this dagger then;
Cassius from bondage will deliver Cassius.
Therein, ye gods, you make the weak most strong;
Therein, ye gods, you tyrants do defeat:
Nor stony tower, nor walls of beaten brass,
Nor airless dungeon, nor strong links of iron,
Can be retentive to the strength of spirit;
But life, being weary of these worldly bars,
Never lacks power to dismiss itself.
If I know this, know all the world besides,
That part of tyranny that I do bear
I can shake off at pleasure.

[*Thunder still*]

CASCA.
                    So can I:
So every bondman in his own hand bears
The power to cancel his captivity.

CASSIUS. And why should Cæsar be a tyrant then?
Poor man! I know he would not be a wolf,
But that he sees the Romans are but sheep:
He were no lion, were not Romans hinds.
Those that with haste will make a mighty fire
Begin it with weak straws: what trash is Rome,
What rubbish and what offal, when it serves
For the base matter to illuminate
So vile a thing as Cæsar! But, O grief,
Where hast thou led me? I perhaps speak this

Before a willing bondman; then I know
My answer must be made. But I am arm'd,
And dangers are to me indifferent.

CASCA. You speak to Casca, and to such a man
That is no fleering tell-tale. Hold, my hand:
Be factious for redress of all these griefs,
And I will set this foot of mine as far
As who goes farthest.

CASSIUS.
                      There's a bargain made.
Now know you, Casca, I have mov'd already
Some certain of the noblest-minded Romans
To undergo with me an enterprise
Of honourable-dangerous consequence;
And I do know, by this they stay for me
In Pompey's porch: for now, this fearful night,
There is no stir or walking in the streets,
And the complexion of the element
In favour's like the work we have in hand,
Most bloody, fiery, and most terrible.

Enter CINNA.

CASCA. Stand close awhile, for here comes one in haste.

CASSIUS. 'Tis Cinna; I do know him by his gait;
He is a friend. Cinna, where haste you so?

CINNA. To find out you. Who's that? Metellus Cimber?

CASSIUS. No, it is Casca; one incorporate
To our attempts. Am I not stay'd for, Cinna?

CINNA. I'm glad on't. What a fearful night is this!
There's two or three of us have seen strange sights.

CASSIUS. Am I not stay'd for? tell me.

CINNA.

                              Yes, you are.
O, Cassius, if you could
But win the noble Brutus to our party —

CASSIUS. Be you content. Good Cinna, take this paper,
And look you lay it in the prætor's chair,
Where Brutus may but find it; and throw this
In at his window; set this up with wax
Upon old Brutus' statue: all this done,
Repair to Pompey's porch, where you shall find us.
Is Decius Brutus and Trebonius there?

CINNA. All but Metellus Cimber; and he's gone
To seek you at your house. Well, I will hie,
And so bestow these papers as you bade me.

CASSIUS. That done, repair to Pompey's theatre.

                              [*Exit* CINNA]

Come, Casca, you and I will yet ere day
See Brutus at his house: three parts of him
Is ours already, and the man entire
Upon the next encounter yields him ours.

CASCA. O, he sits high in all the people's hearts;
And that which would appear offence in us,

His countenance, like richest alchemy,
Will change to virtue and to worthiness.

CASSIUS. Him and his worth and our great need of him,
You have right well conceited. Let us go,
For it is after midnight, and ere day
We will awake him and be sure of him.

[Exeunt]

ACT II.

SCENE I. ROME. BRUTUS'S ORCHARD

Enter BRUTUS

BRUTUS. What, Lucius, ho!
I cannot, by the progress of the stars,
Give guess how near to day. Lucius, I say!
I would it were my fault to sleep so soundly.
When, Lucius, when? awake, I say! what, Lucius!

Enter LUCIUS

LUCIUS. Call'd you, my lord?

BRUTUS. Get me a taper in my study, Lucius:
When it is lighted, come and call me here.

LUCIUS. I will, my lord.

[*Exit*]

BRUTUS. It must be by his death: and, for my part,
I know no personal cause to spurn at him,
But for the general. He would be crown'd:
How that might change his nature, there's the question.
It is the bright day that brings forth the adder,
And that craves wary walking. Crown him? — that; —
And then, I grant, we put a sting in him,
That at his will he may do danger with.
Th' abuse of greatness is when it disjoins
Remorse from power; and, to speak truth of Cæsar,
I have not known when his affections sway'd

More than his reason. But 'tis a common proof,
That lowliness is young ambition's ladder,
Whereto the climber upward turns his face;
But when he once attains the upmost round,
He then unto the ladder turns his back,
Looks in the clouds, scorning the base degrees
By which he did ascend. So Cæsar may;
Then, lest he may, prevent. And, since the quarrel
Will bear no colour for the thing he is,
Fashion it thus; that what he is, augmented,
Would run to these and these extremities;
And therefore think him as a serpent's egg
Which, hatch'd, would, as his kind, grow mischievous,
And kill him in the shell.

Re-enter LUCIUS

LUCIUS. The taper burneth in your closet, sir.
Searching the window for a flint, I found
This paper, thus seal'd up; and I am sure
It did not lie there when I went to bed.

[*Gives him the letter*]

BRUTUS. Get you to bed again; it is not day.
Is not to-morrow, boy, the first of March?

LUCIUS. I know not, sir.

BRUTUS. Look in the calendar, and bring me word.

LUCIUS. I will, sir.

[*Exit*]

BRUTUS. The exhalations whizzing in the air
Give so much light that I may read by them.

[*Opens the letter and reads*]

Brutus, thou sleep'st: awake, and see thyself.
Shall Rome, etc. Speak, strike, redress!
Brutus, thou sleep'st: awake!
Such instigations have been often dropp'd
Where I have took them up.
'Shall Rome, etc.' Thus must I piece it out:
Shall Rome stand under one man's awe? What, Rome?
My ancestors did from the streets of Rome
The Tarquin drive, when he was call'd a king.
'Speak, strike, redress!' Am I entreated
To speak and strike? O Rome, I make thee promise,
If the redress will follow, thou receivest
Thy full petition at the hand of Brutus!

Re-enter[22] LUCIUS

LUCIUS. Sir, March is wasted fifteen days.

[*Knocking within*]

BRUTUS. 'T is good. Go to the gate; somebody knocks.

[*Exit* LUCIUS]

Since Cassius first did whet me against Cæsar,
I have not slept.

Between the acting of a dreadful thing
And the first motion, all the interim is
Like a phantasma or a hideous dream:
The Genius and the mortal instruments
Are then in council; and the state of a man,
Like to a little kingdom, suffers then
The nature of an insurrection.

Re-enter[22] LUCIUS

LUCIUS. Sir, 't is your brother Cassius at the door,
Who doth desire to see you.

BRUTUS.
Is he alone?

LUCIUS. No, sir, there are moe with him.

BRUTUS.
Do you know them?

LUCIUS. No, sir; their hats are pluck'd about their ears,
And half their faces buried in their cloaks,
That by no means I may discover them
By any mark of favour.

BRUTUS.
Let 'em enter.

[*Exit* LUCIUS[34]]

They are the faction. O conspiracy,
Sham'st thou to show thy dangerous brow by night,
When evils are most free? O, then, by day
Where wilt thou find a cavern dark enough
To mask thy monstrous visage? Seek none, conspiracy;

Hide it in smiles and affability:
For if thou path, thy native semblance on,
Not Erebus itself were dim enough
To hide thee from prevention.

CASSIUS. I think we are too bold upon your rest:
Good morrow, Brutus; do we trouble you?

BRUTUS. I have been up this hour, awake all night.
Know I these men that come along with you?

CASSIUS. Yes, every man of them; and no man here
But honours you; and every one doth wish
You had but that opinion of yourself
Which every noble Roman bears of you.
This is Trebonius.

BRUTUS.
                    He is welcome hither.

CASSIUS. This, Decius Brutus.

BRUTUS.
                    He is welcome too.

CASSIUS. This, Casca; this, Cinna; and this, Metellus Cimber.

BRUTUS. They are all welcome.
What watchful cares do interpose themselves
Betwixt your eyes and night?

CASSIUS. Shall I entreat a word?

[*They whisper*]

DECIUS. Here lies the east: doth not the day break here?

CASCA. No.

CINNA. O, pardon, sir, it doth; and yon grey lines
That fret the clouds are messengers of day.

CASCA. You shall confess that you are both deceiv'd.
Here, as I point my sword, the sun arises,
Which is a great way growing on the south,
Weighing the youthful season of the year.
Some two months hence up higher toward the north
He first presents his fire, and the high east
Stands, as the Capitol, directly here.

BRUTUS. Give me your hands all over, one by one.

CASSIUS. And let us swear our resolution.

BRUTUS. No, not an oath: if not the face of men,
The sufferance of our souls, the time's abuse, —
If these be motives weak, break off betimes,
And every man hence to his idle bed;
So let high-sighted tyranny range on,
Till each man drop by lottery. But if these,
As I am sure they do, bear fire enough
To kindle cowards and to steel with valour
The melting spirits of women, then, countrymen,
What need we any spur but our own cause
To prick us to redress? what other bond

Than secret Romans, that have spoke the word,
And will not palter? and what other oath
Than honesty to honesty engag'd,
That this shall be, or we will fall for it?
Swear priests and cowards and men cautelous,
Old feeble carrions and such suffering souls
That welcome wrongs; unto bad causes swear
Such creatures as men doubt; but do not stain
The even virtue of our enterprise,
Nor th' insuppressive mettle of our spirits,
To think that or our cause or our performance
Did need an oath; when every drop of blood
That every Roman bears, and nobly bears,
Is guilty of a several bastardy,
If he do break the smallest particle
Of any promise that hath pass'd from him.

CASSIUS. But what of Cicero? shall we sound him?
I think he will stand very strong with us.

CASCA. Let us not leave him out.

CINNA.
                              No, by no means.

METELLUS. O, let us have him, for his silver hairs
Will purchase us a good opinion,
And buy men's voices to commend our deeds:
It shall be said, his judgment rul'd our hands;
Our youths and wildness shall no whit appear,
But all be buried in his gravity.

BRUTUS. O, name him not; let us not break with him,
For he will never follow any thing

That other men begin.

CASSIUS.

Then leave him out.

CASCA. Indeed he is not fit.

DECIUS. Shall no man else be touch'd but only Cæsar?

CASSIUS. Decius, well urg'd: I think it is not meet,
Mark Antony, so well belov'd of Cæsar,
Should outlive Cæsar: we shall find of him
A shrewd contriver; and, you know, his means,
If he improve them, may well stretch so far
As to annoy us all; which to prevent,
Let Antony and Cæsar fall together.

BRUTUS. Our course will seem too bloody, Caius Cassius,
To cut the head off and then hack the limbs,
Like wrath in death and envy afterwards;
For Antony is but a limb of Cæsar.
Let's be sacrificers, but not butchers, Caius.
We all stand up against the spirit of Cæsar,
And in the spirit of men there is no blood:
O, that we then could come by Cæsar's spirit,
And not dismember Cæsar! But, alas,
Cæsar must bleed for it! And, gentle friends,
Let's kill him boldly, but not wrathfully;
Let's carve him as a dish fit for the gods,
Not hew him as a carcass fit for hounds:
And let our hearts, as subtle masters do,
Stir up their servants to an act of rage,
And after seem to chide 'em . This shall make
Our purpose necessary and not envious;

Which so appearing to the common eyes,
We shall be call'd purgers, not murderers.
And for Mark Antony, think not of him;
For he can do no more than Cæsar's arm
When Cæsar's head is off.

CASSIUS.
                                        Yet I fear him,
For in the ingrafted love he bears to Cæsar —

BRUTUS. Alas, good Cassius, do not think of him:
If he love Cæsar, all that he can do
Is to himself, take thought and die for Cæsar:
And that were much he should, for he is given
To sports, to wildness, and much company.

TREBONIUS. There is no fear in him; let him not die;
For he will live, and laugh at this hereafter.

                                        [*Clock strikes*]

BRUTUS. Peace! count the clock.

CASSIUS.
                            The clock hath stricken three.

TREBONIUS. 'Tis time to part.

CASSIUS.
                            But it is doubtful yet
Whether Cæsar will come forth to-day or no;
For he is superstitious grown of late,
Quite from the main opinion he held once

Of fantasy, of dreams, and ceremonies:
It may be these apparent prodigies,
The unaccustom'd terror of this night,
And the persuasion of his augurers,
May hold him from the Capitol to-day.

DECIUS. Never fear that: if he be so resolv'd,
I can o'ersway him; for he loves to hear
That unicorns may be betray'd with trees,
And bears with glasses, elephants with holes,
Lions with toils, and men with flatterers:
But when I tell him he hates flatterers,
He says he does, being then most flattered.
Let me work;
For I can give his humour the true bent,
And I will bring him to the Capitol.

CASSIUS. Nay, we will all of us be there to fetch him.

BRUTUS. By the eighth hour; is that the uttermost?
CINNA. Be that the uttermost, and fail not then.

METELLUS. Caius Ligarius doth bear Cæsar hard ,
Who rated him for speaking well of Pompey:
I wonder none of you have thought of him.

BRUTUS. Now, good Metellus, go along by him:
He loves me well, and I have given him reasons;
Send him but hither, and I'll fashion him.

CASSIUS. The morning comes upon 's: we'll leave you, Brutus:
And, friends, disperse yourselves; but all remember
What you have said, and show yourselves true Romans.

BRUTUS. Good gentlemen, look fresh and merrily;
Let not our looks put on our purposes;
But bear it as our Roman actors do,
With untir'd spirits and formal constancy:
And so, good morrow to you every one.

[*Exeunt all but* BRUTUS]

Boy! Lucius! Fast asleep? It is no matter;
Enjoy the honey-heavy dew of slumber:
Thou hast no figures nor no fantasies,
Which busy care draws in the brains of men;
Therefore thou sleep'st so sound.

Enter PORTIA

PORTIA.
Brutus, my lord!

BRUTUS. Portia, what mean you? wherefore rise you now?
It is not for your health thus to commit
Your weak condition to the raw cold morning.
PORTIA. Nor for yours neither. You've ungently, Brutus,
Stole from my bed: and yesternight at supper
You suddenly arose, and walk'd about,
Musing and sighing, with your arms across;
And when I ask'd you what the matter was,
You star'd upon me with ungentle looks:
I urg'd you further; then you scratch'd your head,
And too impatiently stamp'd with your foot:
Yet I insisted, yet you answer'd not,
But with an angry wafture of your hand
Gave sign for me to leave you. So I did,
Fearing to strengthen that impatience
Which seem'd too much enkindled, and withal

Hoping it was but an effect of humour,
Which sometime hath his hour with every man.
It will not let you eat, nor talk, nor sleep,
And, could it work so much upon your shape
As it hath much prevail'd on your condition,
I should not know you, Brutus. Dear my lord,
Make me acquainted with your cause of grief.

BRUTUS. I am not well in health, and that is all.

PORTIA. Brutus is wise, and, were he not in health,
He would embrace the means to come by it.

BRUTUS. Why, so I do. Good Portia, go to bed.

PORTIA. Is Brutus sick? and is it physical
To walk unbraced and suck up the humours
Of the dank morning? What, is Brutus sick,
And will he steal out of his wholesome bed,
To dare the vile contagion of the night,
And tempt the rheumy and unpurged air
To add unto his sickness? No, my Brutus;
You have some sick offence within your mind,
Which by the right and virtue of my place
I ought to know of: and, upon my knees,
I charm you, by my once-commended beauty,
By all your vows of love and that great vow
Which did incorporate and make us one,
That you unfold to me, yourself, your half,
Why you are heavy, and what men to-night
Have had resort to you; for here have been
Some six or seven, who did hide their faces
Even from darkness.

BRUTUS.

Kneel not, gentle Portia.

PORTIA. I should not need, if you were gentle Brutus.

Within the bond of marriage, tell me, Brutus,

Is it excepted I should know no secrets

That appertain to you? Am I yourself

But, as it were, in sort or limitation,

To keep with you at meals, comfort your bed,

And talk to you sometimes? Dwell I but in the suburbs

Of your good pleasure? If it be no more,

Portia is Brutus' harlot, not his wife.

BRUTUS. You are my true and honourable wife,

As dear to me as are the ruddy drops

That visit my sad heart.

PORTIA. If this were true, then should I know this secret.

I grant I am a woman; but withal

A woman that Lord Brutus took to wife:

I grant I am a woman; but withal

A woman well-reputed, Cato's daughter.

Think you I am no stronger than my sex,

Being so father'd and so husbanded?

Tell me your counsels; I will not disclose 'em.

I have made strong proof of my constancy,

Giving myself a voluntary wound

Here, in the thigh: can I bear that with patience,

And not my husband's secrets?

BRUTUS.

O ye gods,

Render me worthy of this noble wife!

[*Knocking within*]

Hark, hark! one knocks. Portia, go in a while;
And by and by thy bosom shall partake
The secrets of my heart:
All my engagements I will construe to thee,
All the charactery of my sad brows.
Leave me with haste.

[*Exit* PORTIA]

Lucius, who's that knocks?

Re-enter LUCIUS *with* LIGARIUS

LUCIUS. Here is a sick man that would speak with you.

BRUTUS. Caius Ligarius, that Metellus spake of.
Boy, stand aside. Caius Ligarius! how?

LIGARIUS. Vouchsafe good morrow from a feeble tongue.

BRUTUS. O, what a time have you chose out, brave Caius,
To wear a kerchief! Would you were not sick!

LIGARIUS. I am not sick, if Brutus have in hand
Any exploit worthy the name of honour.

BRUTUS. Such an exploit have I in hand, Ligarius,
Had you a healthful ear to hear of it.

LIGARIUS. By all the gods that Romans bow before,
I here discard my sickness! Soul of Rome!
Brave son, deriv'd from honourable loins!
Thou, like an exorcist, hast conjur'd up

My mortified spirit. Now bid me run,
And I will strive with things impossible;
Yea, get the better of them. What's to do?

BRUTUS. A piece of work that will make sick men whole.

LIGARIUS. But are not some whole that we must make sick?

BRUTUS. That must we also. What it is, my Caius,
I shall unfold to thee, as we are going
To whom it must be done.

LIGARIUS.
                                    Set on your foot,
And with a heart new-fir'd I follow you,
To do I know not what; but it sufficeth
That Brutus leads me on.

BRUTUS.
                                    Follow me, then.

                                                            [*Exeunt*]

The Ides of March

Oil on canvas by Edward John Poynter, 1883.

SCENE II. CÆSAR'S HOUSE

Thunder and lightning. Enter CÆSAR, *in his night-gown*

CÆSAR. Nor heaven nor earth have been at peace to-night:
Thrice hath Calpurnia in her sleep cried out,
'Help, ho! they murder Cæsar!' Who's within?

Enter a Servant

SERVANT. My lord?

CÆSAR. Go bid the priests do present sacrifice,
And bring me their opinions of success.

SERVANT. I will, my lord.

[*Exit*]

Enter CALPURNIA

CALPURNIA. What mean you, Cæsar? think you to walk forth?
You shall not stir out of your house to-day.

CÆSAR. Cæsar shall forth: the things that threaten'd me
Ne'er look'd but on my back; when they shall see
The face of Cæsar, they are vanished.

CALPURNIA. Cæsar, I never stood on ceremonies,
Yet now they fright me. There is one within,
Besides the things that we have heard and seen,
Recounts most horrid sights seen by the watch.

A lioness hath whelped in the streets;
And graves have yawn'd, and yielded up their dead;
Fierce fiery warriors fight upon the clouds,
In ranks and squadrons and right form of war,
Which drizzled blood upon the Capitol;
The noise of battle hurtled in the air,
Horses did neigh, and dying men did groan;
And ghosts did shriek and squeal about the streets.
O Cæsar, these things are beyond all use,
And I do fear them!

CÆSAR.
                    What can be avoided
Whose end is purpos'd by the mighty gods?
Yet Cæsar shall go forth; for these predictions
Are to the world in general as to Cæsar.

CALPURNIA. When beggars die, there are no comets seen;
The heavens themselves blaze forth the death of princes.

CÆSAR. Cowards die many times before their deaths;
The valiant never taste of death but once.
Of all the wonders that I yet have heard,
It seems to me most strange that men should fear;
Seeing that death, a necessary end,
Will come when it will come.

Re-enter Servant

                    What say the augurers?
SERVANT. They would not have you to stir forth to-day.
Plucking the entrails of an offering forth,
They could not find a heart within the beast.

CÆSAR. The gods do this in shame of cowardice:
Cæsar should be a beast without a heart,
If he should stay at home to-day for fear.
No, Cæsar shall not: danger knows full well
That Cæsar is more dangerous than he:
We are two lions litter'd in one day,
And I the elder and more terrible;
And Cæsar shall go forth.

CALPURNIA.
                    Alas, my lord,
Your wisdom is consum'd in confidence!
Do not go forth to-day: call it my fear
That keeps you in the house, and not your own.
We'll send Mark Antony to the senate-house,
And he shall say you are not well to-day:
Let me, upon my knee, prevail in this.

CÆSAR. Mark Antony shall say I am not well;
And, for thy humour, I will stay at home.

                    Enter DECIUS
Here's Decius Brutus, he shall tell them so.

DECIUS. Cæsar, all hail! good morrow, worthy Cæsar:
I come to fetch you to the senate-house.

CÆSAR. And you are come in very happy time,
To bear my greeting to the senators
And tell them that I will not come to-day.
Cannot, is false, and that I dare not, falser;
I will not come to-day. Tell them so, Decius.

CALPURNIA. Say he is sick.

CÆSAR.

Shall Cæsar send a lie?
Have I in conquest stretch'd mine arm so far,
To be afeard to tell graybeards the truth?
Decius, go tell them Cæsar will not come.

DECIUS. Most mighty Cæsar, let me know some cause,
Lest I be laugh'd at when I tell them so.

CÆSAR. The cause is in my will; I will not come;
That is enough to satisfy the senate.
But, for your private satisfaction,
Because I love you, I will let you know:
Calpurnia here, my wife, stays me at home.
She dreamt to-night she saw my statue ,
Which, like a fountain with an hundred spouts,
Did run pure blood; and many lusty Romans
Came smiling and did bathe their hands in it:
And these does she apply for warnings and portents
And evils imminent, and on her knee
Hath begg'd that I will stay at home to-day.

DECIUS. This dream is all amiss interpreted:
It was a vision fair and fortunate.
Your statue spouting blood in many pipes,
In which so many smiling Romans bath'd,
Signifies that from you great Rome shall suck
Reviving blood, and that great men shall press
For tinctures, stains, relics, and cognizance.
This by Calpurnia's dream is signified.

CÆSAR. And this way have you well expounded it.

DECIUS. I have, when you have heard what I can say;
And know it now: the senate have concluded
To give this day a crown to mighty Cæsar.
If you shall send them word you will not come,
Their minds may change. Besides, it were a mock
Apt to be render'd, for some one to say
'Break up the senate till another time,
When Cæsar's wife shall meet with better dreams.'
If Cæsar hide himself, shall they not whisper,
'Lo, Cæsar is afraid'?
Pardon me, Cæsar; for my dear dear love
To your proceeding bids me tell you this;
And reason to my love is liable.

CÆSAR. How foolish do your fears seem now, Calpurnia!
I am ashamed I did yield to them.
Give me my robe, for I will go.

Enter PUBLIUS
BRUTUS, LIGARIUS, METELLUS, CASCA, TREBONIUS, *and* CINNA

And look where Publius is come to fetch me.
PUBLIUS. Good morrow, Cæsar.

CÆSAR.
                    Welcome, Publius.
What, Brutus, are you stirr'd so early too?
Good morrow, Casca. Caius Ligarius,
Cæsar was ne'er so much your enemy
As that same ague which hath made you lean.
What is 't o'clock?

BRUTUS.
                    Cæsar, 't is strucken eight.

CÆSAR. I thank you for your pains and courtesy.

Enter ANTONY

See! Antony, that revels long o' nights,
Is notwithstanding up. Good morrow, Antony.

ANTONY. So to most noble Cæsar.

CÆSAR.
                 Bid them prepare within:
I am to blame to be thus waited for.
Now, Cinna; now, Metellus: what, Trebonius!
I have an hour's talk in store for you;
Remember that you call on me to-day.
Be near me, that I may remember you.

TREBONIUS. Cæsar, I will. [*Aside*] And so near will I be,
That your best friends shall wish I had been further.

CÆSAR. Good friends, go in and taste some wine with me;
And we, like friends, will straightway go together.

BRUTUS. [*Aside*] That every like is not the same, O Cæsar,
The heart of Brutus yearns to think upon!
                                   [*Exeunt*]

SCENE III. *A STREET NEAR THE CAPITOL*

Enter ARTEMIDORUS, *reading a paper*

ARTEMIDORUS. Cæsar, beware of Brutus; take heed of Cassius; come not near Casca; have an eye to Cinna; trust not Trebonius; mark well Metellus Cimber; Decius Brutus loves thee not; thou hast wrong'd Caius Ligarius. There is but one mind in all these men, and it is bent against Cæsar. If thou beest not immortal, look about you: security gives way to conspiracy. The mighty gods defend thee!

Thy lover, ARTEMIDORUS.

Here will I stand till Cæsar pass along,
And as a suitor will I give him this.
My heart laments that virtue cannot live
Out of the teeth of emulation.
If thou read this, O Cæsar, thou mayest live;
If not, the Fates with traitors do contrive.

[Exit]

SCENE IV. *ANOTHER PART OF THE SAME STREET, BEFORE THE HOUSE OF* BRUTUS

Enter PORTIA and LUCIUS

PORTIA. I prithee, boy, run to the senate-house;
Stay not to answer me, but get thee gone.
Why dost thou stay?

LUCIUS.
               To know my errand, madam.
PORTIA. I would have had thee there, and here again,
Ere I can tell thee what thou shouldst do there.
O constancy, be strong upon my side!
Set a huge mountain 'tween my heart and tongue!

I have a man's mind, but a woman's might.
How hard it is for women to keep counsel!
Art thou here yet?

LUCIUS.

Madam, what should I do?
Run to the Capitol, and nothing else?
And so return to you, and nothing else?

PORTIA. Yes, bring me word, boy, if thy lord look well,
For he went sickly forth: and take good note
What Cæsar doth, what suitors press to him.
Hark, boy! what noise is that?

LUCIUS. I hear none, madam.

PORTIA.

Prithee, listen well:
I heard a bustling rumour, like a fray,
And the wind brings it from the Capitol.
LUCIUS. Sooth, madam, I hear nothing.

Enter the SOOTHSAYER

PORTIA. Come hither, fellow: which way hast thou been?

SOOTHSAYER. At mine own house, good lady.

PORTIA. What is 't o'clock?

SOOTHSAYER.

About the ninth hour, lady.

PORTIA. Is Cæsar yet gone to the Capitol?

SOOTHSAYER. Madam, not yet: I go to take my stand,
To see him pass on to the Capitol.

PORTIA. Thou hast some suit to Cæsar, hast thou not?

SOOTHSAYER. That I have, lady: if it will please Cæsar
To be so good to Cæsar as to hear me,
I shall beseech him to befriend himself.

PORTIA. Why, know'st thou any harm's intended towards him?

SOOTHSAYER. None that I know will be, much that I fear may
            chance.
Good morrow to you. Here the street is narrow:
The throng that follows Cæsar at the heels,
Of senators, of prætors, common suitors,
Will crowd a feeble man almost to death:
I'll get me to a place more void, and there
Speak to great Cæsar as he comes along.

ACT III.

SCENE I. ROME. BEFORE THE CAPITOL; THE SENATE SITTING

A crowd of people; among them ARTEMIDORUS *and the*
Soothsayer. *Flourish. Enter* CÆSAR, BRUTUS, CASSIUS,
CASCA, DECIUS, METELLUS, TREBONIUS, CINNA,
ANTONY, LEPIDUS, POPILIUS, PUBLIUS, *and others*

CÆSAR. The Ides of March are come.

SOOTHSAYER. Ay, Cæsar; but not gone.

ARTEMIDORUS. Hail, Cæsar! read this schedule.

DECIUS. Trebonius doth desire you to o'er-read,
At your best leisure, this his humble suit.

ARTEMIDORUS. O Cæsar, read mine first; for mine's a suit
That touches Cæsar nearer: read it, great Cæsar.

CÆSAR. What touches us ourself shall be last serv'd.

ARTEMIDORUS. Delay not, Cæsar; read it instantly.

CÆSAR. What, is the fellow mad?

PUBLIUS.
                    Sirrah, give place.

CASSIUS. What, urge you your petitions in the street?

Come to the Capitol.

CÆSAR *goes up to the Senate-house, the rest following*

POPILIUS. I wish your enterprise to-day may thrive.

CASSIUS. What enterprise, Popilius?

POPILIUS.
                              Fare you well.

                                        [*Advances to* CÆSAR]

BRUTUS. What said Popilius Lena?

CASSIUS. He wish'd to-day our enterprise might thrive.
I fear our purpose is discovered.

BRUTUS. Look, how he makes to Cæsar: mark him.

CASSIUS. Casca, be sudden, for we fear prevention.
Brutus, what shall be done? If this be known,
Cassius or Cæsar never shall turn back,
For I will slay myself.

BRUTUS.
                    Cassius, be constant:
Popilius Lena speaks not of our purposes;
For, look, he smiles, and Cæsar doth not change.

CASSIUS. Trebonius knows his time; for, look you, Brutus,
He draws Mark Antony out of the way.

DECIUS. Where is Metellus Cimber? Let him go,
And presently prefer his suit to Cæsar.

BRUTUS. He is address'd: press near and second him.

CINNA. Casca, you are the first that rears your hand.

CÆSAR. Are we all ready? What is now amiss
That Cæsar and his senate must redress?

METELLUS. Most high, most mighty, and most puissant Cæsar,
Metellus Cimber throws before thy seat
An humble heart,—

[*Kneeling*]

CÆSAR. I must prevent thee, Cimber.
These couchings and these lowly courtesies
Might fire the blood of ordinary men,
And turn pre-ordinance and first decree
Into the law of children. Be not fond,
To think that Cæsar bears such rebel blood
That will be thaw'd from the true quality
With that which melteth fools, I mean, sweet words,
Low-crooked curtsies, and base spaniel-fawning.
Thy brother by decree is banished:
If thou dost bend and pray and fawn for him,
I spurn thee like a cur out of my way.
Know, Cæsar doth not wrong, nor without cause
Will he be satisfied.

METELLUS. Is there no voice more worthy than my own,
To sound more sweetly in great Cæsar's ear

For the repealing of my banish'd brother?

BRUTUS. I kiss thy hand, but not in flattery, Cæsar,
Desiring thee that Publius Cimber may
Have an immediate freedom of repeal.

CÆSAR. What, Brutus!

CASSIUS.
                    Pardon, Cæsar; Cæsar, pardon:
As low as to thy foot doth Cassius fall,
To beg enfranchisement for Publius Cimber.

CÆSAR. I could be well mov'd, if I were as you;
If I could pray to move, prayers would move me:
But I am constant as the northern star,
Of whose true-fix'd and resting quality
There is no fellow in the firmament.
The skies are painted with unnumber'd sparks;
They are all fire and every one doth shine;
But there's but one in all doth hold his place:
So in the world; 'tis furnish'd well with men,
And men are flesh and blood, and apprehensive;
Yet in the number I do know but one
That unassailable holds on his rank,
Unshak'd of motion: and that I am he,
Let me a little show it, even in this;
That I was constant Cimber should be banish'd,
And constant do remain to keep him so.
CINNA. O Cæsar, —

CÆSAR.
                    Hence! wilt thou lift up Olympus?
DECIUS. Great Cæsar, —

CÆSAR.
                    Doth not Brutus bootless kneel?

CASCA. Speak, hands, for me!

                                        [*They stab Cæsar*]

CÆSAR. *Et tu, Brute*? Then fall, Cæsar!

                                            [*Dies*]

CINNA. Liberty! Freedom! Tyranny is dead!
Run hence, proclaim, cry it about the streets.

CASSIUS. Some to the common pulpits, and cry out,
'Liberty, freedom, and enfranchisement!'

BRUTUS. People, and senators, be not affrighted;
Fly not; stand still: ambition's debt is paid.

CASCA. Go to the pulpit, Brutus.

DECIUS. And Cassius too.

BRUTUS. Where's Publius?

CINNA. Here, quite confounded with this mutiny.

METELLUS. Stand fast together, lest some friend of Cæsar's
Should chance —

BRUTUS. Talk not of standing. Publius, good cheer;
There is no harm intended to your person,

Nor to no Roman else: so tell them, Publius.

CASSIUS. And leave us, Publius; lest that the people,
Rushing on us, should do your age some mischief.
BRUTUS. Do so; and let no man abide this deed
But we the doers.

Re-enter TREBONIUS

CASSIUS. Where is Antony?

TREBONIUS.
                    Fled to his house amaz'd.
Men, wives, and children stare, cry out, and run
As it were doomsday.

BRUTUS.
                    Fates, we will know your pleasures:
That we shall die, we know; 'tis but the time,
And drawing days out, that men stand upon.
CASCA . Why, he that cuts off twenty years of life
Cuts off so many years of fearing death.

BRUTUS. Grant that, and then is death a benefit:
So we are Cæsar's friends, that have abridg'd
His time of fearing death. Stoop, Romans, stoop,
And let us bathe our hands in Cæsar's blood
Up to the elbows, and besmear our swords:
Then walk we forth, even to the market-place,
And, waving our red weapons o'er our heads,
Let's all cry 'Peace, freedom, and liberty!'

CASSIUS. Stoop, then, and wash. How many ages hence
Shall this our lofty scene be acted over

In states unborn and accents yet unknown!

BRUTUS. How many times shall Cæsar bleed in sport,
That now on Pompey's basis lies along
No worthier than the dust!

CASSIUS.
                    So oft as that shall be,
So often shall the knot of us be call'd
The men that gave their country liberty.

DECIUS. What, shall we forth?

CASSIUS.
                    Ay, every man away:
Brutus shall lead; and we will grace his heels
With the most boldest and best hearts of Rome.

Enter a Servant

BRUTUS. Soft! who comes here? A friend of Antony's.

SERVANT. Thus, Brutus, did my master bid me kneel;
Thus did Mark Antony bid me fall down;
And, being prostrate, thus he bade me say:
Brutus is noble, wise, valiant, and honest;
Cæsar was mighty, bold, royal, and loving:
Say I love Brutus and I honour him;
Say I fear'd Cæsar, honour'd him, and lov'd him.
If Brutus will vouchsafe that Antony
May safely come to him, and be resolv'd
How Cæsar hath deserv'd to lie in death,
Mark Antony shall not love Cæsar dead
So well as Brutus living; but will follow

The fortunes and affairs of noble Brutus
Thorough the hazards of this untrod state
With all true faith. So says my master Antony.

BRUTUS. Thy master is a wise and valiant Roman;
I never thought him worse.
Tell him, so please him come unto this place,
He shall be satisfied, and, by my honour,
Depart untouch'd.

SERVANT.
                I'll fetch him presently.

                                                      [*Exit*]

BRUTUS. I know that we shall have him well to friend.

CASSIUS. I wish we may: but yet have I a mind
That fears him much, and my misgiving still
Falls shrewdly to the purpose.

Re-enter ANTONY

BRUTUS. But here comes Antony. Welcome, Mark Antony.

ANTONY. O mighty Cæsar! dost thou lie so low?
Are all thy conquests, glories, triumphs, spoils,
Shrunk to this little measure? Fare thee well!
I know not, gentlemen, what you intend,
Who else must be let blood, who else is rank:
If I myself, there is no hour so fit
As Cæsar's death's hour, nor no instrument
Of half that worth as those your swords, made rich

With the most noble blood of all this world.
I do beseech ye, if you bear me hard,
Now, whilst your purpled hands do reek and smoke,
Fulfil your pleasure. Live a thousand years,
I shall not find myself so apt to die:
No place will please me so, no mean of death,
As here by Cæsar, and by you cut off,
The choice and master spirits of this age.

BRUTUS. O Antony, beg not your death of us.
Though now we must appear bloody and cruel,
As, by our hands and this our present act,
You see we do; yet see you but our hands
And this the bleeding business they have done:
Our hearts you see not; they are pitiful;
And pity to the general wrong of Rome—
As fire drives out fire, so pity pity—
Hath done this deed on Cæsar. For your part,
To you our swords have leaden points, Mark Antony:
Our arms in strength of malice, and our hearts
Of brothers' temper, do receive you in
With all kind love, good thoughts, and reverence.

CASSIUS. Your voice shall be as strong as any man's
In the disposing of new dignities.

BRUTUS. Only be patient till we have appeas'd
The multitude, beside themselves with fear,
And then we will deliver you the cause
Why I, that did love Cæsar when I struck him,
Have thus proceeded.

ANTONY.
                    I doubt not of your wisdom.

Let each man render me his bloody hand:
First, Marcus Brutus, will I shake with you;
Next, Caius Cassius, do I take your hand;
Now, Decius Brutus, yours; now yours, Metellus;
Yours, Cinna; and, my valiant Casca, yours;
Though last, not least in love, yours, good Trebonius.
Gentlemen all,—alas, what shall I say?
My credit now stands on such slippery ground,
That one of two bad ways you must conceit me,
Either a coward or a flatterer.
That I did love thee, Cæsar, O, 'tis true:
If, then, thy spirit look upon us now,
Shall it not grieve thee dearer than thy death,
To see thy Antony making his peace,
Shaking the bloody fingers of thy foes,
Most noble! in the presence of thy corse?
Had I as many eyes as thou hast wounds,
Weeping as fast as they stream forth thy blood,
It would become me better than to close
In terms of friendship with thine enemies.
Pardon me, Julius! Here wast thou bay'd, brave hart;
Here didst thou fall, and here thy hunters stand,
Sign'd in thy spoil and crimson'd in thy lethe .
O world, thou wast the forest to this hart;
And this, indeed, O world, the heart of thee.
How like a deer, strucken by many princes,
Dost thou here lie!

CASSIUS.
     Mark Antony,—

ANTONY.
        Pardon me, Caius Cassius:
The enemies of Cæsar shall say this;

Then, in a friend, it is cold modesty.

CASSIUS. I blame you not for praising Cæsar so;
But what compact mean you to have with us?
Will you be prick'd in number of our friends,
Or shall we on, and not depend on you?

ANTONY. Therefore I took your hands, but was indeed
Sway'd from the point by looking down on Cæsar.
Friends am I with you all, and love you all,
Upon this hope that you shall give me reasons
Why and wherein Cæsar was dangerous.

BRUTUS. Or else were this a savage spectacle:
Our reasons are so full of good regard
That, were you, Antony, the son of Cæsar,
You should be satisfied.

ANTONY.
                    That's all I seek:
And am moreover suitor that I may
Produce his body to the market-place;
And in the pulpit, as becomes a friend,
Speak in the order of his funeral.

BRUTUS. You shall, Mark Antony.

CASSIUS.
                    Brutus, a word with you.
[*Aside to* BRUTUS] You know not what you do; do not consent
That Antony speak in his funeral:
Know you how much the people may be mov'd
By that which he will utter?

BRUTUS.

By your pardon:
I will myself into the pulpit first,
And show the reason of our Cæsar's death:
What Antony shall speak, I will protest
He speaks by leave and by permission,
And that we are contented Cæsar shall
Have all true rites and lawful ceremonies.
It shall advantage more than do us wrong.

CASSIUS. I know not what may fall; I like it not.

BRUTUS. Mark Antony, here, take you Cæsar's body.
You shall not in your funeral speech blame us,
But speak all good you can devise of Cæsar,
And say you do 't by our permission;
Else shall you not have any hand at all
About his funeral: and you shall speak
In the same pulpit whereto I am going,
After my speech is ended.

ANTONY.

Be it so;
I do desire no more.

BRUTUS. Prepare the body, then, and follow us.

[*Exeunt all but* ANTONY]

ANTONY. O, pardon me, thou bleeding piece of earth,
That I am meek and gentle with these butchers!
Thou art the ruins of the noblest man
That ever lived in the tide of times.

Woe to the hand that shed this costly blood!
Over thy wounds now do I prophesy,
Which, like dumb mouths, do ope their ruby lips,
To beg the voice and utterance of my tongue,
A curse shall light upon the limbs of men;
Domestic fury and fierce civil strife
Shall cumber all the parts of Italy;
Blood and destruction shall be so in use,
And dreadful objects so familiar,
That mothers shall but smile when they behold
Their infants quartered with the hands of war;
All pity chok'd with custom of fell deeds:
And Cæsar's spirit, ranging for revenge,
With Ate by his side come hot from hell,
Shall in these confines with a monarch's voice
Cry 'Havoc,' and let slip the dogs of war;
That this foul deed shall smell above the earth
With carrion men, groaning for burial.

Enter a Servant

You serve Octavius Cæsar, do you not?

SERVANT. I do, Mark Antony.

ANTONY. Cæsar did write for him to come to Rome.

SERVANT. He did receive his letters, and is coming;
  And bid me say to you by word of mouth —
  O Cæsar!

[*Seeing the body*]

ANTONY. Thy heart is big; get thee apart and weep.
Passion, I see, is catching; for mine eyes,
Seeing those beads of sorrow stand in thine,
Began to water. Is thy master coming?

SERVANT. He lies to-night within seven leagues of Rome.

ANTONY. Post back with speed, and tell him what hath chanc'd.
Here is a mourning Rome, a dangerous Rome,
No Rome of safety for Octavius yet;
Hie hence, and tell him so. Yet stay awhile;
Thou shalt not back till I have borne this corse
Into the market-place: there shall I try,
In my oration, how the people take
The cruel issue of these bloody men;
According to the which, thou shalt discourse
To young Octavius of the state of things.
Lend me your hand.

[*Exeunt with* CÆSAR'S *body*]

SCENE II. *THE FORUM*

Enter BRUTUS *and* CASSIUS, *and a throng of* Citizens

CITIZENS. We will be satisfied; let us be satisfied.

BRUTUS. Then follow me, and give me audience, friends.
Cassius, go you into the other street,
And part the numbers.
Those that will hear me speak, let 'em stay here;
Those that will follow Cassius, go with him;
And public reasons shall be rendered

Of Cæsar's death.

1 CITIZEN. I will hear Brutus speak.

2 CITIZEN. I will hear Cassius; and compare their reasons,
When severally we hear them rendered[107].

[*Exit* CASSIUS, *with some of the* Citizens. BRUTUS *goes into the pulpit*]

3 CITIZEN. The noble Brutus is ascended: silence!

BRUTUS. Be patient till the last.

Romans, countrymen, and lovers! hear me for my cause, and be silent, that you may hear: believe me for mine honour, and have respect to mine honour, that you may believe: censure me in your wisdom, and awake your senses, that you may the better judge. If there be any in this assembly, any dear friend of Cæsar's, to him I say that Brutus' love to Cæsar was no less than his. If then that friend demand why Brutus rose against Cæsar, this is my answer: Not that I lov'd Cæsar less, but that I lov'd Rome more. Had you rather Cæsar were living, and die all slaves, than that Cæsar were dead, to live all free-men? As Cæsar lov'd me, I weep for him; as he was fortunate, I rejoice at it; as he was valiant, I honour him: but as he was ambitious, I slew him. There is tears for his love; joy for his fortune; honour for his valour; and death for his ambition. Who is here so base that would be a bondman? If any, speak; for him have I offended. Who is here so rude that would not be a Roman? If any, speak; for him have I offended. Who is here so vile that will not love his country? If any, speak; for him have I offended. I pause for a reply.

ALL. None, Brutus, none.

BRUTUS. Then none have I offended. I have done no more to Cæsar than you shall do to Brutus. The question of his death is enroll'd in the Capitol; his glory not extenuated, wherein he was worthy, nor his offences enforc'd, for which he suffer'd death.

Enter ANTONY *and others, with* CÆSAR'S *body*

Here comes his body, mourn'd by Mark Antony; who, though he had no hand in his death, shall receive the benefit of his dying, a place in the commonwealth; as which of you shall not? With this I depart, — that, as I slew my best lover for the good of Rome, I have the same dagger for myself, when it shall please my country to need my death.

ALL. Live, Brutus! live, live!

1 CITIZEN. Bring him with triumph home unto his house.

2 CITIZEN. Give him a statue with his ancestors.

3 CITIZEN. Let him be Cæsar.

4 CITIZEN.
                    Cæsar's better parts
Shall be crown'd in Brutus.

1 CITIZEN. We'll bring him to his house with shouts and clamours.

BRUTUS. My countrymen, —

2 CITIZEN.

Peace! silence! Brutus speaks.

1 CITIZEN. Peace, ho!

BRUTUS. Good countrymen, let me depart alone,
And, for my sake, stay here with Antony:
Do grace to Cæsar's corpse, and grace his speech
Tending to Cæsar's glories; which Mark Antony,
By our permission, is allow'd to make.
I do entreat you, not a man depart,
Save I alone, till Antony have spoke.

[*Exit*]

1 CITIZEN. Stay, ho! and let us hear Mark Antony.

3 CITIZEN. Let him go up into the public chair;
We'll hear him. Noble Antony, go up.

ANTONY. For Brutus' sake, I am beholding to you.
4 CITIZEN. What does he say of Brutus?

3 CITIZEN.
                              He says, for Brutus' sake,
He finds himself beholding to us all.

4 CITIZEN. 'Twere best he speak no harm of Brutus here.

1 CITIZEN. This Cæsar was a tyrant.

3 CITIZEN.
                              Nay, that's certain:
We are blest that Rome is rid of him.

2 CITIZEN. Peace! let us hear what Antony can say.

ANTONY. You gentle Romans, —

ALL.

                              Peace, ho! Let us hear him.

ANTONY. Friends, Romans, countrymen, lend me your ears:
I come to bury Cæsar, not to praise him.
The evil that men do lives after them:
The good is oft interred with their bones;
So let it be with Cæsar. The noble Brutus
Hath told you Cæsar was ambitious:
If it were so, it was a grievous fault,
And grievously hath Cæsar answer'd it.
Here, under leave of Brutus and the rest, —
For Brutus is an honourable man;
So are they all, all honourable men, —
Come I to speak in Cæsar's funeral.
He was my friend, faithful and just to me:
But Brutus says he was ambitious;
And Brutus is an honourable man.
He hath brought many captives home to Rome,
Whose ransoms did the general coffers fill:
Did this in Cæsar seem ambitious?
When that the poor have cried, Cæsar hath wept:
Ambition should be made of sterner stuff:
Yet Brutus says he was ambitious;
And Brutus is an honourable man.
You all did see that on the Lupercal
I thrice presented him a kingly crown,
Which he did thrice refuse: was this ambition?
Yet Brutus says he was ambitious;
And, sure, he is an honourable man.
I speak not to disprove what Brutus spoke,
But here I am to speak what I do know.

You all did love him once, not without cause:
What cause withholds you then to mourn for him?
O judgment! thou art fled to brutish beasts,
And men have lost their reason. Bear with me;
My heart is in the coffin there with Cæsar,
And I must pause till it come back to me.

1 CITIZEN. Methinks there is much reason in his sayings.

2 CITIZEN. If thou consider rightly of the matter,
Cæsar has had great wrong.
3 CITIZEN.
                    Has he, masters?
I fear there will a worse come in his place.

4 CITIZEN. Mark'd ye his words? He would not take the crown;
Therefore 'tis certain he was not ambitious.

1 CITIZEN. If it be found so, some will dear abide it.

2 CITIZEN. Poor soul! his eyes are red as fire with weeping.

3 CITIZEN. There's not a nobler man in Rome than Antony.

4 CITIZEN. Now mark him; he begins again to speak.

ANTONY. But yesterday the word of Cæsar might
Have stood against the world: now lies he there,
And none so poor to do him reverence.
O masters, if I were dispos'd to stir
Your hearts and minds to mutiny and rage,
I should do Brutus wrong and Cassius wrong,
Who, you all know, are honourable men:
I will not do them wrong; I rather choose

To wrong the dead, to wrong myself and you,
Than I will wrong such honourable men.
But here's a parchment with the seal of Cæsar;
I found it in his closet; 'tis his will:
Let but the commons hear this testament—
Which, pardon me, I do not mean to read—
And they would go and kiss dead Cæsar's wounds,
And dip their napkins in his sacred blood,
Yea, beg a hair of him for memory,
And, dying, mention it within their wills,
Bequeathing it as a rich legacy
Unto their issue.

4 CITIZEN. We'll hear the will: read it, Mark Antony.

ALL. The will, the will! we will hear Cæsar's will.

ANTONY. Have patience, gentle friends, I must not read it;
It is not meet you know how Cæsar lov'd you.
You are not wood, you are not stones, but men;
And, being men, hearing the will of Cæsar,
It will inflame you, it will make you mad.
'T is good you know not that you are his heirs;
For if you should, O, what would come of it!

4 CITIZEN. Read the will; we'll hear it, Antony;
You shall read us the will, Cæsar's will.

ANTONY. Will you be patient? will you stay awhile?
I have o'ershot myself to tell you of it:
I fear I wrong the honourable men
Whose daggers have stabb'd Cæsar; I do fear it.

4 CITIZEN. They were traitors: honourable men!

ALL. The will! the testament!

2 CITIZEN. They were villains, murderers: the will! read the will.

ANTONY. You will compel me, then, to read the will?
Then make a ring about the corpse of Cæsar,
And let me show you him that made the will.
Shall I descend? and will you give me leave?

ALL. Come down.

2 CITIZEN. Descend.

3 CITIZEN. You shall have leave.

[ANTONY *comes down from the pulpit*]

4 CITIZEN. A ring, stand round.

1 CITIZEN. Stand from the hearse, stand from the body.

2 CITIZEN. Room for Antony, most noble Antony.

ANTONY. Nay, press not so upon me: stand far off.

ALL. Stand back; room; bear back!

ANTONY. If you have tears, prepare to shed them now.
You all do know this mantle: I remember
The first time ever Cæsar put it on;
'Twas on a summer's evening, in his tent,
That day he overcame the Nervii.
Look, in this place ran Cassius' dagger through:

See what a rent the envious Casca made:
Through this the well-beloved Brutus stabb'd;
And, as he pluck'd his cursed steel away,
Mark how the blood of Cæsar follow'd it,
As rushing out of doors, to be resolv'd
If Brutus so unkindly knock'd, or no;
For Brutus, as you know, was Cæsar's angel:
Judge, O you gods, how dearly Cæsar lov'd him!
This was the most unkindest cut of all;
For when the noble Cæsar saw him stab,
Ingratitude, more strong than traitors' arms,
Quite vanquish'd him: then burst his mighty heart;
And, in his mantle muffling up his face,
Even at the base of Pompey's statue,
Which all the while ran blood, great Cæsar fell.
O, what a fall was there, my countrymen!
Then I, and you, and all of us fell down,
Whilst bloody treason flourish'd over us.
O, now you weep; and I perceive you feel
The dint of pity: these are gracious drops.
Kind souls, what, weep you when you but behold
Our Cæsar's vesture wounded? Look you here,
Here is himself, marr'd, as you see, with traitors.

1 CITIZEN. O piteous spectacle!

2 CITIZEN. O noble Cæsar!

3 CITIZEN. O woful day!

4 CITIZEN. O traitors, villains!

1 CITIZEN. O most bloody sight!

2 CITIZEN. We will be reveng'd.

ALL. Revenge! About! Seek! Burn! Fire! Kill! Slay! Let not a traitor live!

ANTONY. Stay, countrymen.

1 CITIZEN. Peace there! Hear the noble Antony.

2 CITIZEN. We'll hear him, we'll follow him, we'll die with him.

ANTONY. Good friends, sweet friends, let me not stir you up
To such a sudden flood of mutiny.
They that have done this deed are honourable;
What private griefs they have, alas, I know not,
That made them do it; they are wise and honourable,
And will, no doubt, with reasons answer you.
I come not, friends, to steal away your hearts:
I am no orator, as Brutus is;
But, as you know me all, a plain blunt man,
That love my friend; and that they know full well
That gave me public leave to speak of him:
For I have neither wit , nor words, nor worth,
Action, nor utterance, nor the power of speech,
To stir men's blood: I only speak right on;
I tell you that which you yourselves do know;
Show you sweet Cæsar's wounds, poor poor dumb mouths,

And bid them speak for me: but were I Brutus,
And Brutus Antony, there were an Antony
Would ruffle up your spirits, and put a tongue
In every wound of Cæsar, that should move
The stones of Rome to rise and mutiny.

ALL. We'll mutiny.

1 CITIZEN. We'll burn the house of Brutus.

3 CITIZEN. Away, then! come, seek the conspirators.

ANTONY. Yet hear me, countrymen; yet hear me speak.

ALL. Peace, ho! hear Antony, most noble Antony!

ANTONY. Why, friends, you go to do you know not what.
Wherein hath Cæsar thus deserv'd your loves?
Alas, you know not; I must tell you then:
You have forgot the will I told you of.

ALL. Most true. The will! Let's stay and hear the will.

ANTONY. Here is the will, and under Cæsar's seal.
To every Roman citizen he gives,
To every several man, seventy-five drachmas.

2 CITIZEN. Most noble Cæsar! We'll revenge his death.

3 CITIZEN. O royal Cæsar!

ANTONY. Hear me with patience.

ALL. Peace, ho!

ANTONY. Moreover, he hath left you all his walks,
His private arbours and new-planted orchards,
On this side Tiber; he hath left them you,
And to your heirs for ever; common pleasures,
To walk abroad and recreate yourselves.
Here was a Cæsar! when comes such another?

1 CITIZEN. Never, never. Come, away, away!
We'll burn his body in the holy place,
And with the brands fire the traitors' houses.
Take up the body.

2 CITIZEN. Go fetch fire.

3 CITIZEN. Pluck down benches.

4 CITIZEN. Pluck down forms, windows, any thing.

[*Exeunt* CITIZENS *with the body*]

ANTONY. Now let it work. Mischief, thou art afoot,
Take thou what course thou wilt!

Enter a Servant

How now, fellow!

SERVANT. Sir, Octavius is already come to Rome.

ANTONY. Where is he?

SERVANT. He and Lepidus are at Cæsar's house.

ANTONY. And thither will I straight to visit him:
He comes upon a wish. Fortune is merry,
And in this mood will give us any thing.

SERVANT. I heard him say, Brutus and Cassius
Are rid like madmen through the gates of Rome.

ANTONY. Belike they had some notice of the people
How I had mov'd them. Bring me to Octavius.

[*Exeunt*]

SCENE III. *A STREET*

Enter CINNA *the poet*

CINNA. I dreamt to-night that I did feast with Cæsar,
And things unluckily charge my fantasy:
I have no will to wander forth of doors,

Yet something leads me forth.

Enter CITIZENS

1 CITIZEN. What is your name?

2 CITIZEN. Whither are you going?

3 CITIZEN. Where do you dwell?

4 CITIZEN. Are you a married man or a bachelor?

2 CITIZEN. Answer every man directly.

1 CITIZEN. Ay, and briefly.

4 CITIZEN. Ay, and wisely.

3 CITIZEN. Ay, and truly, you were best.

CINNA. What is my name? Whither[169] am I going? Where do I dwell? Am I a married man or a bachelor? Then, to answer every man directly and briefly, wisely and truly: wisely I say, I am a bachelor.

2 CITIZEN. That's as much as to say, they are fools that marry: you'll bear me a bang for that, I fear. Proceed; directly.

CINNA. Directly, I am going to Cæsar's funeral.

1 CITIZEN. As a friend or an enemy?

CINNA. As a friend.

2 CITIZEN. That matter is answered directly.

4 CITIZEN. For your dwelling, briefly.

CINNA. Briefly, I dwell by the Capitol.

3 CITIZEN. Your name, sir, truly.

CINNA. Truly, my name is Cinna.

1 CITIZEN. Tear him to pieces; he's a conspirator.

CINNA. I am Cinna the poet, I am Cinna the poet.

4 CITIZEN. Tear him for his bad verses, tear him for his bad verses.

CINNA. I am not Cinna the conspirator.

4 CITIZEN. It is no matter, his name's Cinna; pluck but his name out of his heart, and turn him going.

3 CITIZEN. Tear him, tear him! Come, brands, ho! firebrands! to Brutus', to Cassius'; burn all: some to Decius' house, and some to Casca's; some to Ligarius': away, go!

[Exeunt]

ACT IV

SCENE I. *ROME. A ROOM IN* ANTONY'S *HOUSE*

ANTONY, OCTAVIUS, *and* LEPIDUS, *seated at a table*

ANTONY. These many then shall die; their names are prick'd.

OCTAVIUS. Your brother too must die; consent you, Lepidus?
LEPIDUS. I do consent—

OCTAVIUS.
               Prick him down, Antony.

LEPIDUS. Upon condition Publius shall not live,
Who is your sister's son, Mark Antony.

ANTONY. He shall not live; look, with a spot I damn him.
But, Lepidus, go you to Cæsar's house;
Fetch the will hither, and we shall determine
How to cut off some charge in legacies.

LEPIDUS. What, shall I find you here?

OCTAVIUS. Or here, or at the Capitol.

                                     [*Exit* LEPIDUS]

ANTONY. This is a slight unmeritable man,
Meet to be sent on errands: is it fit,
The three-fold world divided, he should stand
One of the three to share it?

OCTAVIUS.

                    So you thought him;
And took his voice who should be prick'd to die,
In our black sentence and proscription.

ANTONY. Octavius, I have seen more days than you:
And though we lay these honours on this man,
To ease ourselves of divers slanderous loads,
He shall but bear them as the ass bears gold,
To groan and sweat under the business,
Either led or driven, as we point the way;
And having brought our treasure where we will,
Then take we down his load and turn him off,
Like to the empty ass, to shake his ears
And graze in commons.

OCTAVIUS.

                    You may do your will;
But he's a tried and valiant soldier.

ANTONY. So is my horse, Octavius; and for that
I do appoint him store of provender:
It is a creature that I teach to fight,
To wind, to stop, to run directly on,
His corporal motion govern'd by my spirit.
And, in some taste, is Lepidus but so;
He must be taught, and train'd, and bid go forth:
A barren-spirited fellow; one that feeds
On objects, arts, and imitations,
Which, out of use and stal'd by other men,
Begin his fashion: do not talk of him

But as a property. And now, Octavius,
Listen great things: Brutus and Cassius
Are levying powers: we must straight make head:
Therefore let our alliance be combin'd,
Our best friends made, and our best means stretch'd out ;
And let us presently go sit in council,
How covert matters may be best disclos'd,
And open perils surest answered.

OCTAVIUS. Let us do so: for we are at the stake,
And bay'd about with many enemies;
And some that smile have in their hearts, I fear,
Millions of mischiefs.

[*Exeunt*]

SCENE II. *BEFORE* BRUTUS'S *TENT, IN THE CAMP NEAR* SARDIS

Drum. Enter BRUTUS, TITINIUS, LUCIUS, *and* Soldiers;
LUCILIUS *and* PINDARUS *meet them*

BRUTUS. Stand, ho!

LUCILIUS. Give the word, ho! and stand.

BRUTUS. What now, Lucilius! is Cassius near?

LUCILIUS. He is at hand; and Pindarus is come
To do you salutation from his master.

[PINDARUS *gives a letter to* BRUTUS]

BRUTUS. He greets me well. Your master, Pindarus,
In his own change , or by ill officers,
Hath given me some worthy cause to wish
Things done undone: but, if he be at hand,
I shall be satisfied.

PINDARUS. I do not doubt
But that my noble master will appear
Such as he is, full of regard and honour.

BRUTUS. He is not doubted. A word, Lucilius,
How he receiv'd you : let me be resolv'd.

LUCILIUS. With courtesy and with respect enough;
But not with such familiar instances,
Nor with such free and friendly conference,
As he hath us'd of old.

BRUTUS.
                    Thou hast describ'd
A hot friend cooling: ever note, Lucilius,
When love begins to sicken and decay,
It useth an enforced ceremony.
There are no tricks in plain and simple faith:
But hollow men, like horses hot at hand,
Make gallant show and promise of their mettle;
But when they should endure the bloody spur,
They fall their crests, and, like deceitful jades,
Sink in the trial. Comes his army on?

LUCILIUS. They mean this night in Sardis to be quarter'd;
The greater part, the horse in general,

Are come with Cassius.

[*Low march within*]

BRUTUS.
Hark! he is arriv'd.
March gently on to meet him.

Enter CASSIUS *and his Powers*

CASSIUS. Stand, ho!

BRUTUS. Stand, ho! Speak the word along.

1 SOLDIER. Stand!

2 SOLDIER. Stand!

3 SOLDIER. Stand!

CASSIUS. Most noble brother, you have done me wrong.

BRUTUS. Judge me, you gods! wrong I mine enemies?
And, if not so, how should I wrong a brother?

CASSIUS. Brutus, this sober form of yours hides wrongs;
And when you do them—

BRUTUS.

Cassius, be content;
Speak your griefs softly: I do know you well.
Before the eyes of both our armies here,
Which should perceive nothing but love from us,
Let us not wrangle: bid them move away;
Then in my tent, Cassius, enlarge your griefs,
And I will give you audience.

CASSIUS.
Pindarus,
Bid our commanders lead their charges off
A little from this ground.

BRUTUS. Lucilius, do you the like; and let no man
Come to our tent till we have done our conference.
Let Lucius and Titinius guard our door.

[Exeunt]

Brutus and the Ghost of Caesar

Copperplate engraving by E. Scriven from a painting by Richard Westall, 1802.

Scene III. Brutus's *Tent*

Enter Brutus *and* Cassius

CASSIUS. That you have wrong'd me doth appear in this:
You have condemn'd and noted Lucius Pella
For taking bribes here of the Sardians;
Wherein my letters, praying on his side,
Because I knew the man, was slighted off.

BRUTUS. You wrong'd yourself to write in such a case.

CASSIUS. In such a time as this it is not meet
That every nice offence should bear his comment.

BRUTUS. Let me tell you, Cassius, you yourself
Are much condemn'd to have an itching palm,
To sell and mart your offices for gold
To undeservers.

CASSIUS.
               I an itching palm!
You know that you are Brutus that speaks this,
Or, by the gods, this speech were else your last.

BRUTUS. The name of Cassius honours this corruption,
And chastisement doth therefore hide his head.

CASSIUS. Chastisement!

BRUTUS. Remember March, the Ides of March remember:
Did not great Julius bleed for justice' sake?
What villain touch'd his body, that did stab,
And not for justice? What! shall one of us,

That struck the foremost man of all this world
But for supporting robbers, shall we now
Contaminate our fingers with base bribes,
And sell the mighty space of our large honours
For so much trash as may be grasped thus?
I had rather be a dog, and bay the moon,
Than such a Roman.
CASSIUS.

           Brutus, bait not me;
I'll not endure it. You forget yourself,
To hedge me in; I am a soldier, I,
Older in practice, abler than yourself
To make conditions.

BRUTUS.

           Go to ; you are not, Cassius.

CASSIUS. I am.

BRUTUS. I say you are not.

CASSIUS. Urge me no more, I shall forget myself;
Have mind upon your health, tempt me no farther.

BRUTUS. Away, slight man!
CASSIUS. Is't possible?

BRUTUS.

           Hear me, for I will speak.
Must I give way and room to your rash choler?
Shall I be frighted when a madman stares?

CASSIUS. O ye gods, ye gods! must I endure all this?

BRUTUS. All this! ay, more: fret till your proud heart break;
Go show your slaves how choleric you are,
And make your bondmen tremble. Must I budge?
Must I observe you? must I stand and crouch
Under your testy humour? By the gods,
You shall digest the venom of your spleen,
Though it do split you; for, from this day forth,
I'll use you for my mirth, yea, for my laughter,
When you are waspish.

CASSIUS.
                    Is it come to this?

BRUTUS. You say you are a better soldier:
Let it appear so; make your vaunting true,
And it shall please me well: for mine own part,
I shall be glad to learn of noble men.

CASSIUS. You wrong me every way; you wrong me, Brutus;
I said an elder soldier, not a better:
Did I say 'better'?

BRUTUS.
                    If you did, I care not.

CASSIUS. When Cæsar liv'd, he durst not thus have mov'd me.

BRUTUS. Peace, peace! you durst not so have tempted him.

CASSIUS. I durst not!

BRUTUS. No.

CASSIUS. What, durst not tempt him!

BRUTUS.

For your life you durst not.

CASSIUS. Do not presume too much upon my love;
I may do that I shall be sorry for.

BRUTUS. You have done that you should be sorry for.
There is no terror, Cassius, in your threats;
For I am arm'd so strong in honesty,
That they pass by me as the idle wind,
Which I respect not. I did send to you
For certain sums of gold, which you denied me:
For I can raise no money by vile means:
By heaven, I had rather coin my heart,
And drop my blood for drachmas, than to wring
From the hard hands of peasants their vile trash
By any indirection. I did send
To you for gold to pay my legions,
Which you denied me. Was that done like Cassius?
Should I have answer'd Caius Cassius so?
When Marcus Brutus grows so covetous,
To lock such rascal counters from his friends,
Be ready, gods, with all your thunderbolts,
Dash him to pieces!

CASSIUS.

I denied you not.

BRUTUS. You did.

CASSIUS. I did not: he was but a fool that brought
My answer back. Brutus hath riv'd my heart:
A friend should bear his friend's infirmities,
But Brutus makes mine greater than they are.

BRUTUS. I do not, till you practise them on me.

CASSIUS. You love me not.

BRUTUS.
                           I do not like your faults.

CASSIUS. A friendly eye could never see such faults.

BRUTUS. A flatterer's would not, though they do appear
As huge as high Olympus.

CASSIUS. Come, Antony, and young Octavius, come,
Revenge yourselves alone on Cassius,
For Cassius is a-weary of the world;
Hated by one he loves; brav'd by his brother;
Check'd like a bondman; all his faults observ'd,
Set in a note-book, learn'd, and conn'd by rote,
To cast into my teeth. O, I could weep
My spirit from mine eyes! There is my dagger,
And here my naked breast; within, a heart
Dearer than Plutus' mine, richer than gold:
If that thou be'st a Roman, take it forth;
I, that denied thee gold, will give my heart:
Strike, as thou didst at Cæsar; for I know,
When thou didst hate him worst, thou lov'dst him better
Than ever thou lov'dst Cassius.

BRUTUS.
                           Sheathe your dagger:
Be angry when you will, it shall have scope;
Do what you will, dishonour shall be humour .
O Cassius, you are yoked with a lamb
That carries anger as the flint bears fire;

Who, much enforced, shows a hasty spark,
And straight is cold again.

CASSIUS.

Hath Cassius liv'd
To be but mirth and laughter to his Brutus,
When grief and blood ill-temper'd vexeth him?

BRUTUS. When I spoke that, I was ill-temper'd too.

CASSIUS. Do you confess so much? Give me your hand.

BRUTUS. And my heart too.

CASSIUS.

O Brutus!

BRUTUS.

What's the matter?
CASSIUS. Have not you love enough to bear with me,
When that rash humour which my mother gave me
Makes me forgetful?

BRUTUS.

Yes, Cassius; and from henceforth,
When you are over-earnest with your Brutus,
He'll think your mother chides, and leave you so.

POET. [*Within*] Let me go in to see the generals;
There is some grudge between 'em; 'tis not meet
They be alone.

LUCILIUS. [*Within*] You shall not come to them.

POET. [*Within*] Nothing but death shall stay me.

Enter Poet, *followed by* LUCILIUS, TITINIUS, *and* LUCIUS

CASSIUS. How now! what's the matter?

POET. For shame, you generals! what do you mean?
Love, and be friends, as two such men should be;
For I have seen more years, I'm sure, than ye.

CASSIUS. Ha, ha! how vilely doth this cynic rhyme!

BRUTUS. Get you hence, sirrah; saucy fellow, hence!

CASSIUS. Bear with him, Brutus; 'tis his fashion.

BRUTUS. I'll know his humour, when he knows his time:
What should the wars do with these jigging fools?
Companion, hence!

CASSIUS.
                    Away, away, be gone!

                                        [*Exit* Poet]

BRUTUS. Lucilius and Titinius, bid the commanders
Prepare to lodge their companies to-night.

CASSIUS. And come yourselves, and bring Messala with you
Immediately to us.

                    [*Exeunt* LUCILIUS *and* TITINIUS]

BRUTUS.
              Lucius, a bowl of wine!

Cassius. I did not think you could have been so angry.

Brutus. O Cassius, I am sick of many griefs.

Cassius. Of your philosophy you make no use,
If you give place to accidental evils.

Brutus. No man bears sorrow better. Portia is dead.

Cassius. Ha! Portia!

Brutus. She is dead.

Cassius. How 'scaped I killing when I cross'd you so?
O insupportable and touching loss!
Upon what sickness?

Brutus.
               Impatient of my absence,
And grief that young Octavius with Mark Antony
Have made themselves so strong,—for with her death
That tidings came,—with this she fell distract,
And, her attendants absent, swallow'd fire.

Cassius. And died so?

Brutus.
               Even so.

Cassius.
               O ye immortal gods!

Re-enter LUCIUS, *with wine and taper*

BRUTUS. Speak no more of her. Give me a bowl of wine.
In this I bury all unkindness, Cassius.

[*Drinks*]

CASSIUS. My heart is thirsty for that noble pledge.
Fill Lucius, till the wine o'erswell the cup;
I cannot drink too much of Brutus' love.

[*Drinks*]

BRUTUS. Come in, Titinius!

[*Exit* LUCIUS]

Re-enter TITINIUS, *with* MESSALA

Welcome, good Messala.
Now sit we close about this taper here,
And call in question our necessities.

CASSIUS. Portia, art thou gone?

BRUTUS.
No more, I pray you.
Messala, I have here received letters,
That young Octavius and Mark Antony
Come down upon us with a mighty power,
Bending their expedition toward Philippi.

MESSALA. Myself have letters of the selfsame tenour.

BRUTUS. With what addition?

MESSALA. That by proscription and bills of outlawry,
Octavius, Antony, and Lepidus,
Have put to death an hundred senators.

BRUTUS. Therein our letters do not well agree;
Mine speak of seventy senators that died
By their proscriptions, Cicero being one.

CASSIUS. Cicero one!

MESSALA.
                Cicero is dead,
And by that order of proscription
Had you your letters from your wife, my lord?

BRUTUS. No, Messala.

MESSALA. Nor nothing in your letters writ of her?
BRUTUS. Nothing, Messala.

MESSALA.
                        That, methinks, is strange.

BRUTUS. Why ask you? hear you aught of her in yours?

MESSALA. No, my lord.

BRUTUS. Now, as you are a Roman, tell me true.

MESSALA. Then like a Roman bear the truth I tell:
For certain she is dead, and by strange manner.

BRUTUS. Why, farewell, Portia. We must die, Messala:
With meditating that she must die once,

I have the patience to endure it now.

MESSALA. Even so great men great losses should endure.

CASSIUS. I have as much of this in art as you,
But yet my nature could not bear it so.

BRUTUS. Well, to our work alive. What do you think
Of marching to Philippi presently?

CASSIUS. I do not think it good.

BRUTUS.
                              Your reason?

CASSIUS.
                                        This it is:
'Tis better that the enemy seek us:
So shall he waste his means, weary his soldiers,
Doing himself offence; whilst we, lying still,
Are full of rest, defence, and nimbleness.

BRUTUS. Good reasons must of force give place to better.
The people 'twixt Philippi and this ground
Do stand but in a forc'd affection,
For they have grudg'd us contribution:
The enemy, marching along by them,
By them shall make a fuller number up,
Come on refresh'd, new-added , and encourag'd;
From which advantage shall we cut him off
If at Philippi we do face him there,
These people at our back.

CASSIUS.

Hear me, good brother.

BRUTUS. Under your pardon. You must note beside,
That we have tried the utmost of our friends,
Our legions are brim-full, our cause is ripe:
The enemy increaseth every day;
We, at the height, are ready to decline.
There is a tide in the affairs of men,
Which, taken at the flood, leads on to fortune;
Omitted, all the voyage of their life
Is bound in shallows and in miseries.
On such a full sea are we now afloat;
And we must take the current when it serves,
Or lose our ventures.

CASSIUS.
                        Then, with your will, go on;
We'll along ourselves, and meet them at Philippi.

BRUTUS. The deep of night is crept upon our talk,
And nature must obey necessity;
Which we will niggard with a little rest.
There is no more to say?

CASSIUS.
                        No more. Good night:
Early to-morrow will we rise, and hence.

BRUTUS. Lucius! [*Re-enter* LUCIUS] My gown.

                        [*Exit* LUCIUS]. Farewell, good Messala:
Good night, Titinius: noble, noble Cassius,
Good night, and good repose.

CASSIUS.

                    O my dear brother!
This was an ill beginning of the night:
Never come such division 'tween our souls!
Let it not, Brutus.

BRUTUS.

                    Every thing is well.

CASSIUS. Good night, my lord.

BRUTUS.

                    Good night, good brother.

TITINIUS.
                    Good night, Lord Brutus.

MESSALA.

BRUTUS.

                    Farewell, every one.

                    [*Exeunt* CASSIUS, TITINIUS, *and* MESSALA]

                    Re-enter LUCIUS, *with the gown*

Give me the gown. Where is thy instrument?

LUCIUS. Here in the tent.

BRUTUS.
                    What, thou speak'st drowsily?
Poor knave, I blame thee not; thou art o'er-watch'd.
Call Claudius and some other of my men;
I'll have them sleep on cushions in my tent.

LUCIUS. Varro and Claudius!

Enter VARRO *and* CLAUDIUS

VARRO. Calls my lord?

BRUTUS. I pray you, sirs, lie in my tent and sleep;
It may be I shall raise you by-and-by
On business to my brother Cassius.

VARRO. So please you, we will stand and watch your pleasure.

BRUTUS. I will not have it so: lie down, good sirs;
It may be I shall otherwise bethink me.
Look, Lucius, here's the book I sought for so;
I put it in the pocket of my gown.

[VARRO *and* CLAUDIUS *lie down*]

LUCIUS. I was sure your lordship did not give it me.

BRUTUS. Bear with me, good boy, I am much forgetful.
Canst thou hold up thy heavy eyes awhile,
And touch thy instrument a strain or two?

LUCIUS. Ay, my lord, an 't please you.
BRUTUS.
It does, my boy:
I trouble thee too much, but thou art willing.

LUCIUS. It is my duty, sir.

BRUTUS. I should not urge thy duty past thy might;
I know young bloods look for a time of rest.

LUCIUS. I have slept, my lord, already.

BRUTUS. It was well done; and thou shalt sleep again;
I will not hold thee long: if I do live,
I will be good to thee.

[*Music, and a song*]

This is a sleepy tune. O murderous slumber ,
Lay'st thou thy leaden mace upon my boy,
That plays thee music? Gentle knave, good night;
I will not do thee so much wrong to wake thee:
If thou dost nod, thou break'st thy instrument;
I'll take it from thee; and, good boy, good night.
Let me see, let me see; is not the leaf turn'd down
Where I left reading? Here it is, I think.

Enter the Ghost *of* CÆSAR

How ill this taper burns! Ha! who comes here?
I think it is the weakness of mine eyes
That shapes this monstrous apparition.
It comes upon me. Art thou any thing?
Art thou some god, some angel, or some devil,
That mak'st my blood cold, and my hair to stare?
Speak to me what thou art.

GHOST. Thy evil spirit, Brutus.

BRUTUS.
                    Why com'st thou?

GHOST. To tell thee thou shalt see me at Philippi.

BRUTUS. Well; then I shall see thee again?

GHOST. Ay, at Philippi.

Brutus and the Ghost of Cæsar.

Copperplate engraving by Edward Scriven from a painting by
Richard Westall. London, 1802.

BRUTUS. Why, I will see thee at Philippi then.

[*Exit* Ghost]

Now I have taken heart thou vanishest:
Ill spirit, I would hold more talk with thee.
Boy, Lucius! Varro! Claudius! Sirs, awake!
Claudius!

LUCIUS. The strings, my lord, are false.

BRUTUS. He thinks he still is at his instrument.
Lucius, awake!

LUCIUS. My lord?

BRUTUS. Didst thou dream, Lucius, that thou so criedst out?

LUCIUS. My lord, I do not know that I did cry.

BRUTUS. Yes, that thou didst: didst thou see any thing?

LUCIUS. Nothing, my lord.

BRUTUS. Sleep again, Lucius. Sirrah Claudius!
[*To* VARRO] Fellow thou, awake!

VARRO. My lord?

CLAUDIUS. My lord?

BRUTUS. Why did you so cry out, sirs, in your sleep?

VARRO & CLAUDIUS. Did we, my lord?

BRUTUS.

       Ay: saw you any thing?

VARRO. No, my lord, I saw nothing.

CLAUDIUS.

        Nor I, my lord.

BRUTUS. Go and commend me to my brother Cassius;
Bid him set on his powers betimes before,
And we will follow.

VARRO & CLAUDIUS[150]. It shall be done, my lord.

               [Exeunt]

ACT V

SCENE I. *THE PLAINS OF PHILIPPI*

Enter OCTAVIUS, ANTONY, *and their Army*

OCTAVIUS. Now, Antony, our hopes are answered:
You said the enemy would not come down,
But keep the hills and upper regions.
It proves not so: their battles are at hand;
They mean to warn us at Philippi here,
Answering before we do demand of them.

ANTONY. Tut, I am in their bosoms, and I know
Wherefore they do it: they could be content
To visit other places, and come down
With fearful bravery, thinking by this face
To fasten in our thoughts that they have courage;
But 'tis not so.

Enter a Messenger

MESSENGER.
              Prepare you, generals:
The enemy comes on in gallant show;
Their bloody sign of battle is hung out,
And something to be done immediately.

ANTONY. Octavius, lead your battle softly on,
Upon the left hand of the even field.

OCTAVIUS. Upon the right hand I; keep thou the left.

ANTONY. Why do you cross me in this exigent?

OCTAVIUS. I do not cross you; but I will do so.

[*March*]

Drum. Enter BRUTUS, CASSIUS, *and their Army;*
LUCILIUS, TITINIUS, MESSALA, *and others*

BRUTUS. They stand, and would have parley.

CASSIUS. Stand fast, Titinius: we must out and talk.

OCTAVIUS. Mark Antony, shall we give sign of battle?

ANTONY. No, Cæsar, we will answer on their charge.
Make forth; the generals would have some words.

OCTAVIUS. Stir not until the signal.

BRUTUS. Words before blows: is it so, countrymen?

OCTAVIUS. Not that we love words better, as you do.

BRUTUS. Good words are better than bad strokes, Octavius.

ANTONY. In your bad strokes, Brutus, you give good words.
Witness the hole you made in Cæsar's heart,
Crying, 'Long live! hail, Cæsar!'

CASSIUS.
                    Antony,
The posture of your blows are yet unknown;
But, for your words, they rob the Hybla bees,
And leave them honeyless.

ANTONY.
                    Not stingless too.

~ 114 ~

BRUTUS. O, yes, and soundless too;
For you have stol'n their buzzing, Antony,
And very wisely threat before you sting.

ANTONY. Villains, you did not so, when your vile daggers
Hack'd one another in the sides of Cæsar:
You show'd your teeth like apes, and fawn'd like hounds,
And bow'd like bondmen, kissing Cæsar's feet;
Whilst damned Casca, like a cur, behind
Struck Cæsar on the neck. O you flatterers!

CASSIUS. Flatterers! Now, Brutus, thank yourself:
This tongue had not offended so to-day,
If Cassius might have rul'd.

OCTAVIUS. Come, come, the cause: if arguing make us sweat,
The proof of it will turn to redder drops.
Look;
I draw a sword against conspirators;
When think you that the sword goes up again?
Never, till Cæsar's three and thirty wounds
Be well aveng'd; or till another Cæsar
Have added slaughter to the sword of traitors.

BRUTUS. Cæsar, thou canst not die by traitors' hands,
Unless thou bring'st them with thee.

OCTAVIUS.
                        So I hope;
I was not born to die on Brutus' sword.

BRUTUS. O, if thou wert the noblest of thy strain,
Young man, thou couldst not die more honourable.

CASSIUS. A peevish schoolboy, worthless of such honour,
Join'd with a masker and a reveller!

ANTONY. Old Cassius still!

OCTAVIUS.
               Come, Antony; away!
Defiance, traitors, hurl we in your teeth;
If you dare fight to-day, come to the field;
If not, when you have stomachs.

          [*Exeunt* OCTAVIUS, ANTONY, *and their* Army]

CASSIUS. Why, now, blow wind, swell billow, and swim bark!
The storm is up, and all is on the hazard.

BRUTUS. Ho, Lucilius! hark, a word with you.

LUCILIUS. [*Standing forth*] My lord?

          [BRUTUS *and* LUCILIUS *converse apart*]

CASSIUS. Messala!

MESSALA.
        What says my general?

CASSIUS.
            Messala,
This is my birth-day; as this very day
Was Cassius born. Give me thy hand, Messala:
Be thou my witness that, against my will,
As Pompey was, am I compell'd to set

Upon one battle all our liberties.
You know that I held Epicurus strong,
And his opinion: now I change my mind,
And partly credit things that do presage.
Coming from Sardis, on our former ensign
Two mighty eagles fell, and there they perch'd,
Gorging and feeding from our soldiers' hands;
Who to Philippi here consorted us:
This morning are they fled away and gone;
And in their steads do ravens, crows, and kites,
Fly o'er our heads and downward look on us,
As we were sickly prey: their shadows seem
A canopy most fatal, under which
Our army lies, ready to give up the ghost.

MESSALA. Believe not so.

CASSIUS.
                        I but believe it partly;
For I am fresh of spirit, and resolv'd
To meet all perils very constantly.

BRUTUS. Even so, Lucilius.

CASSIUS.
                        Now, most noble Brutus,
The gods to-day stand friendly, that we may,
Lovers in peace, lead on our days to age!
But, since the affairs of men rests still incertain,
Let's reason with the worst that may befall.
If we do lose this battle, then is this
The very last time we shall speak together:
What are you then determined to do?

BRUTUS. Even by the rule of that philosophy
By which I did blame Cato for the death
Which he did give himself: I know not how,
But I do find it cowardly and vile,
For fear of what might fall, so to prevent
The time of life: arming myself with patience
To stay the providence of some high powers
That govern us below.

CASSIUS.

          Then, if we lose this battle,
You are contented to be led in triumph
Thorough the streets of Rome?

BRUTUS. No, Cassius, no: think not, thou noble Roman,
That ever Brutus will go bound to Rome;
He bears too great a mind. But this same day
Must end that work the Ides of March begun;
115And whether we shall meet again I know not.
Therefore our everlasting farewell take.
For ever, and for ever, farewell, Cassius!
If we do meet again, why, we shall smile;
If not, why then this parting was well made.
120CASSIUS. For ever, and for ever, farewell, Brutus!
If we do meet again, we'll smile indeed;
If not, 'tis true this parting was well made.
BRUTUS. Why, then, lead on. O, that a man might know
The end of this day's business ere it come!
125But it sufficeth that the day will end,
And then the end is known. Come, ho! away!

                                 [*Exeunt*]

SCENE II. *THE FIELD OF BATTLE*

Alarum. Enter BRUTUS *and* MESSALA

BRUTUS. Ride, ride, Messala, ride, and give these bills
Unto the legions on the other side:

[*Loud alarum*]

Let them set on at once; for I perceive
But cold demeanour in Octavius' wing,
And sudden push gives them the overthrow.
Ride, ride, Messala: let them all come down.

[*Exeunt*]

SCENE III. *ANOTHER PART OF THE FIELD*

Alarums. Enter CASSIUS *and* TITINIUS

CASSIUS. O, look, Titinius, look, the villains fly!
Myself have to mine own turn'd enemy.
This ensign here of mine was turning back;
I slew the coward, and did take it from him.

TITINIUS. O Cassius, Brutus gave the word too early;
Who, having some advantage on Octavius,
Took it too eagerly: his soldiers fell to spoil,
Whilst we by Antony are all enclos'd.

Enter PINDARUS

PINDARUS. Fly further off, my lord, fly further off;
Mark Antony is in your tents, my lord:
Fly, therefore, noble Cassius, fly far off.

CASSIUS. This hill is far enough. Look, look, Titinius;
Are those my tents where I perceive the fire?

TITINIUS. They are, my lord.

CASSIUS.

                    Titinius, if thou lovest me,
Mount thou my horse, and hide thy spurs in him,
Till he have brought thee up to yonder troops,
And here again; that I may rest assur'd
Whether yond troops are friend or enemy.
TITINIUS. I will be here again, even with a thought.

                                    [*Exit*]

CASSIUS. Go, Pindarus, get higher on that hill;
My sight was ever thick; regard Titinius,
And tell me what thou not'st about the field.

                     [PINDARUS *ascends the hill*]

This day I breathed first: time is come round,
And where I did begin, there shall I end;
My life is run his compass. Sirrah, what news?

PINDARUS. [*Above*] O my lord!

CASSIUS. What news?

PINDARUS. [*Above*] Titinius is enclosed round about
With horsemen, that make to him on the spur;
Yet he spurs on. Now they are almost on him.
Now, Titinius! Now some light. O, he lights too:
He's ta'en. [*Shout*] And, hark! they shout for joy.

CASSIUS. Come down; behold no more.
O, coward that I am, to live so long,
To see my best friend ta'en before my face!

PINDARUS descends

Come hither, sirrah:
In Parthia did I take thee prisoner;
And then I swore thee, saving of thy life,
That whatsoever I did bid thee do,
Thou shouldst attempt it. Come now, keep thine oath;
Now be a freeman; and with this good sword,
That ran through Cæsar's bowels, search this bosom.
Stand not to answer: here, take thou the hilts;
And, when my face is cover'd, as 'tis now,
Guide thou the sword. [PINDARUS *stabs him*] Cæsar, thou art
        reveng'd,
Even with the sword that kill'd thee.

[*Dies*]

PINDARUS. So, I am free; yet would not so have been,
Durst I have done my will. O Cassius!
Far from this country Pindarus shall run,
Where never Roman shall take note of him.

[*Exit*]

Re-enter TITINIUS, *with* MESSALA

MESSALA. It is but change, Titinius; for Octavius
Is overthrown by noble Brutus' power,
As Cassius' legions are by Antony.

TITINIUS. These tidings will well comfort Cassius.

MESSALA. Where did you leave him?

TITINIUS.

                                        All disconsolate,
With Pindarus his bondman, on this hill.

MESSALA. Is not that he that lies upon the ground?

TITINIUS. He lies not like the living. O my heart!

MESSALA. Is not that he?

TITINIUS.

                            No, this was he, Messala,
But Cassius is no more. O setting sun,
As in thy red rays thou dost sink to night,
So in his red blood Cassius' day is set ;
The sun of Rome is set! Our day is gone;
Clouds, dews, and dangers come; our deeds are done!
Mistrust of my success hath done this deed.

MESSALA. Mistrust of good success hath done this deed.
O hateful error, melancholy's child,
Why dost thou show to the apt thoughts of men
The things that are not? O error, soon conceiv'd,
Thou never com'st unto a happy birth,
But kill'st the mother that engender'd thee!

TITINIUS. What, Pindarus! where art thou, Pindarus?

MESSALA. Seek him, Titinius, whilst I go to meet
The noble Brutus, thrusting this report
Into his ears: I may say, 'thrusting' it;
For piercing steel and darts envenomed

Shall be as welcome to the ears of Brutus
As tidings of this sight.

TITINIUS.
                    Hie you, Messala,
And I will seek for Pindarus the while.

                                        [*Exit* MESSALA]

Why didst thou send me forth, brave Cassius?
Did I not meet thy friends? and did not they
Put on my brows this wreath of victory,
And bid me give it thee? Didst thou not hear their shouts?
Alas, thou hast misconstrued every thing!
But, hold thee, take this garland on thy brow;
Thy Brutus bid me give it thee, and I
Will do his bidding. Brutus, come apace,
And see how I regarded Caius Cassius.
By your leave, gods: this is a Roman's part:
90Come, Cassius' sword, and find Titinius' heart.

                                        [*Dies*]

Alarum. Re-enter MESSALA, *with* BRUTUS, *young*
CATO, STRATO, VOLUMNIUS, *and* LUCILIUS

BRUTUS. Where, where, Messala, doth his body lie?

MESSALA. Lo, yonder, and Titinius mourning it.

BRUTUS. Titinius' face is upward.

CATO.
                    He is slain.

BRUTUS. O Julius Cæsar, thou art mighty yet!

Thy spirit walks abroad, and turns our swords
In our own proper entrails.

CATO.

                    Brave Titinius!
Look, where he have not crown'd dead Cassius!

BRUTUS. Are yet two Romans living such as these?
The last of all the Romans, fare thee well!
It is impossible that ever Rome
Should breed thy fellow. Friends, I owe moe tears
To this dead man than you shall see me pay.
I shall find time, Cassius, I shall find time.
Come, therefore, and to Thasos send his body:
His funerals shall not be in our camp,
Lest it discomfort us. Lucilius, come;
And come, young Cato; let us to the field.
Labeo and Flavius , set our battles on:
'T is three o'clock; and, Romans, yet ere night
We shall try fortune in a second fight.

                    [*Exeunt*

SCENE IV. *ANOTHER PART OF THE FIELD.*

Alarum. Enter BRUTUS, *young* CATO, LUCILIUS, *and others*

BRUTUS. Yet, countrymen, O, yet hold up your heads!

CATO. What bastard doth not? Who will go with me?
I will proclaim my name about the field.
I am the son of Marcus Cato, ho!
A foe to tyrants, and my country's friend;
I am the son of Marcus Cato, ho!

Enter Soldiers, *and fight*

LUCILIUS. And I am Brutus, Marcus Brutus, I;
Brutus, my country's friend; know me for Brutus!
O young and noble Cato, art thou down?
Why, now thou diest as bravely as Titinius;
And mayst be honour'd, being Cato's son .

1 SOLDIER. Yield, or thou diest.

LUCILIUS.
                    Only I yield to die:
There is so much that thou wilt kill me straight;

                                        [*Offering money*]

Kill Brutus, and be honour'd in his death.

1 SOLDIER. We must not. A noble prisoner!

2 SOLDIER. Room, ho! Tell Antony, Brutus is ta'en.

1 SOLDIER. I'll tell the news. Here comes the general.

Enter ANTONY

Brutus is ta'en, Brutus is ta'en, my lord.

ANTONY. Where is he?

LUCILIUS. Safe, Antony; Brutus is safe enough:
I dare assure thee that no enemy
Shall ever take alive the noble Brutus:
The gods defend him from so great a shame!
When you do find him, or alive or dead,
He will be found like Brutus, like himself

ANTONY. This is not Brutus, friend; but, I assure you,
A prize no less in worth: keep this man safe,
Give him all kindness: I had rather have
Such men my friends than enemies. Go on,
And see where Brutus be alive or dead;
And bring us word unto Octavius' tent
How every thing is chanc'd.

[Exeunt]

SCENE V. *ANOTHER PART OF THE FIELD*

Enter BRUTUS, DARDANIUS, CLITUS, STRATO, *and* VOLUMNIUS

BRUTUS. Come, poor remains of friends, rest on this rock.

CLITUS. Statilius show'd the torch-light, but, my lord;
He came not back. He is or ta'en or slain.
BRUTUS. Sit thee down, Clitus: slaying is the word;
It is a deed in fashion. Hark thee, Clitus.

[Whispering]

CLITUS. What, I, my lord? No, not for all the world.

BRUTUS. Peace then! no words.

CLITUS.
　　　　　　　　　I'll rather kill myself.

BRUTUS. Hark thee, Dardanius.

[Whispering[112]*]*

DARDANIUS.

~ 126 ~

Shall I do such a deed?

CLITUS. O Dardanius!

DARDANIUS. O Clitus!

CLITUS. What ill request did Brutus make to thee?

DARDANIUS. To kill him, Clitus. Look, he meditates.

CLITUS. Now is that noble vessel full of grief,
That it runs over even at his eyes.

BRUTUS. Come hither, good Volumnius; list a word.

VOLUMNIUS. What says my lord?

BRUTUS.
                Why, this, Volumnius:
The ghost of Cæsar hath appear'd to me
Two several times by night; at Sardis once,
And, this last night, here in Philippi fields:
I know my hour is come.

VOLUMNIUS.
                Not so, my lord.
BRUTUS. Nay, I am sure it is, Volumnius.
Thou seest the world, Volumnius, how it goes;
Our enemies have beat us to the pit:

[Low alarums]

It is more worthy to leap in ourselves
Than tarry till they push us. Good Volumnius,
Thou know'st that we two went to school together:

Even for that our love of old, I prithee,
Hold thou my sword-hilts, whilst I run on it.

VOLUMNIUS. That's not an office for a friend, my lord.

[*Alarum still*]

CLITUS. Fly, fly, my lord; there is no tarrying here.

BRUTUS. Farewell to you; and you; and you, Volumnius.
Strato, thou hast been all this while asleep;
Farewell to thee, too, Strato. Countrymen,
My heart doth joy that yet in all my life
I found no man but he was true to me.
I shall have glory by this losing day,
More than Octavius and Mark Antony
By this vile conquest shall attain unto.
So, fare you well at once; for Brutus' tongue
Hath almost ended his life's history:
Night hangs upon mine eyes; my bones would rest,
That have but labour'd to attain this hour.

[*Alarum. Cry within*, 'Fly, fly, fly!']

CLITUS. Fly, my lord, fly!

BRUTUS.
            Hence! I will follow.

[*Exeunt* CLITUS, DARDANIUS, *and* VOLUMNIUS]

I prithee, Strato, stay thou by thy lord:
Thou art a fellow of a good respect;
Thy life hath had some smatch of honour in it:
Hold then my sword, and turn away thy face,
While I do run upon it. Wilt thou, Strato?

STRATO. Give me your hand first: fare you well, my lord.

BRUTUS. Farewell, good Strato. [*Runs on his sword*]
Cæsar, now be still:
I kill'd not thee with half so good a will.

[*Dies*]

Alarum. Retreat. Enter ANTONY, OCTAVIUS, MESSALA.

LUCILIUS, and the Army

OCTAVIUS. What man is that?

MESSALA. My master's man. Strato, where is thy master?

STRATO. Free from the bondage you are in, Messala:
The conquerors can but make a fire of him;
For Brutus only overcame himself,
And no man else hath honour by his death.

LUCILIUS. So Brutus should be found. I thank thee, Brutus,
That thou hast prov'd Lucilius' saying true.

OCTAVIUS. All that serv'd Brutus, I will entertain them.
Fellow, wilt thou bestow thy time with me?

STRATO. Ay, if Messala will prefer me to you.

OCTAVIUS. Do so, good Messala.

MESSALA. How died my master, Strato?

STRATO. I held the sword, and he did run on it.

MESSALA. Octavius, then take him to follow thee,
That did the latest service to my master.

ANTONY. This was the noblest Roman of them all:
All the conspirators, save only he,
Did that they did in envy of great Cæsar;
He only, in a general honest thought
And common good to all, made one of them.
His life was gentle, and the elements
So mix'd in him, that Nature might stand up
And say to all the world, 'This was a man!'

OCTAVIUS. According to his virtue let us use him,
With all respect and rites of burial.
Within my tent his bones to-night shall lie,
Most like a soldier, ordered honourably.
So call the field to rest; and let's away
To part the glories of this happy day.

[*Exeunt*]

FINIS.

STUDENT NOTES

The Tragedy of Julius Caesar is a tragedy by William Shakespeare, believed to have been written in 1599. It is one of several plays written by Shakespeare based on true events from Roman history, which also include Coriolanus and Antony and Cleopatra.

Although the title is Julius Caesar, Caesar is not the most visible character in its action, appearing alive in only three scenes. Marcus Brutus speaks more than four times as many lines, and the central psychological drama of the play focuses on Brutus' struggle between the conflicting demands of honour, patriotism and friendship.

CHARACTERS

Julius Caesar

Triumvirs after Caesar's death

Octavius Caesar

Mark Antony

Lepidus

Conspirators against Caesar

Marcus Brutus (Brutus)

Cassius

Casca

Decius Brutus

Cinna

Metellus Cimber

Trebonius

Caius Ligarius

Tribunes

Flavius

Marullus

Roman Senate Senators

Cicero

Publius

Popilius Lena

Citizens

Calpurnia – Caesar's wife

Portia – Brutus' wife

Soothsayer

Artemidorus – sophist from Knidos

Cinna – poet

Cobbler

Carpenter

Poet (believed to be based on Marcus Favonius)

Lucius – Brutus' attendant

Loyal to Brutus and Cassius

Volumnius

Titinius

Young Cato – Portia's brother

Messala – messenger

Varrus

Clitus

Claudio

Dardanius

Strato

Lucilius

Labeo (non-speaking role)

Flavius (non-speaking role)

Statilius (non-speaking role)

Pindarus – Cassius' bondman

Other

Caesar's servant

Antony's servant

Octavius' servant

Messenger

Other soldiers, senators, plebeians, and attendants

SYNOPSIS

The play opens with the commoners of Rome celebrating Caesar's triumphant return from defeating Pompey's sons at the battle of Munda. Two tribunes, Flavius and Marrullus, discover the commoners celebrating, insult them for their change in loyalty from Pompey to Caesar, and break up the crowd. They also plan on removing all decorations from Caesar's statues and ending any other festivities. In the next scene, during Caesar's parade on the feast of Lupercal, a soothsayer warns Caesar to "Beware the ides of March", a warning he disregards. The action then turns to the discussion between Brutus and Cassius. In this conversation, Cassius attempts to influence Brutus' opinions into believing Caesar should be killed, preparing to have Brutus join his conspiracy to kill Caesar. They then hear from Casca that Mark Antony has offered Caesar the crown of Rome three times, and that each time Caesar refused it, fainting after the last refusal. Later, in act two, Brutus joins the conspiracy, although after much moral debate, eventually deciding that Caesar, although his friend and never having done anything against the people of Rome, should be killed to prevent him from doing anything against the people of Rome if he were ever to be crowned. He compares Caesar to "A serpents egg/ which hatch'd, would, as his kind, grow mischievous,/ and kill him in the shell.", and decides to join Cassius in killing Caesar.

Caesar's assassination is one of the most famous scenes of the play, occurring in Act 3, scene 1. After ignoring the soothsayer, as well as his wife's own premonitions, Caesar comes to the Senate. The conspirators create a superficial motive for coming close enough to assassinate Caesar by means of a petition brought by Metellus Cimber, pleading on behalf of his banished brother. As Caesar, predictably, rejects the petition, Casca grazes Caesar in the back of his neck, and the others follow in stabbing him; Brutus is last. At this point, Shakespeare makes Caesar utter the famous line "Et tu, Brute?" ("And you, Brutus?", i.e. "You too, Brutus?"). Shakespeare has him add, "Then fall, Caesar," suggesting that such treachery destroyed Caesar's will to live.

The conspirators make clear that they committed this act for Rome, not for their own purposes, and do not attempt to flee the scene. After Caesar's death, Brutus delivers an oration defending his actions, and for the moment, the crowd is on his side. However, Mark Antony, with a subtle and eloquent speech over Caesar's corpse—beginning with the much-quoted Friends, Romans, countrymen, lend me your ears—deftly turns public opinion against the assassins by manipulating the emotions of the common people, in contrast to the rational tone of Brutus's speech, yet there is method in his rhetorical speech and gestures: he reminds them of the good Caesar had done for Rome, his sympathy with the poor, and his refusal of the crown at the Lupercal, thus questioning Brutus' claim of Caesar's ambition; he shows Caesar's bloody, lifeless body to the crowd to have them shed tears and gain sympathy for their fallen hero; and he reads Caesar's will, in which every Roman citizen would receive 75 drachmas. Antony, even as he states his intentions against it, rouses the mob to drive the conspirators from Rome. Amid the violence, an innocent poet, Cinna, is confused with the conspirator Lucius Cinna and is murdered by the mob.

The beginning of Act Four is marked by the quarrel scene, where Brutus attacks Cassius for soiling the noble act of regicide by accepting bribes ("Did not great Julius bleed for justice' sake? / What villain touch'd his body, that did stab, / And not for justice?") The two are reconciled, especially after Brutus reveals that his beloved wife Portia had committed suicide under the stress of his absence from Rome; they prepare for a war against Mark Antony and Caesar's adopted son, Octavius. That night, Caesar's ghost appears to Brutus with a warning of defeat ("thou shalt see me at Philippi").

At the battle, Cassius and Brutus, knowing that they will probably both die, smile their last smiles to each other and hold hands. During the battle, Cassius has his servant Pindarus kill him after hearing of the capture of his best friend, Titinius. After Titinius, who was not really captured, sees Cassius's corpse, he commits suicide. However, Brutus wins that stage of the battle - but his victory is not conclusive. With a heavy heart, Brutus battles again the next day. He loses and commits suicide by running on his own sword, which is held by a soldier named Strato.

The play ends with a tribute to Brutus by Antony, who proclaims that Brutus has remained "the noblest Roman of them all" because he was the only conspirator who acted, in his mind, for the good of Rome. There is then a small hint at the friction between Mark Antony and Octavius which will characterize another of Shakespeare's Roman plays, Antony and Cleopatra.

SOURCES

The main source of the play is Thomas North's translation of Plutarch's Lives.

Deviations from Plutarch[edit]

Shakespeare makes Caesar's triumph take place on the day of Lupercalia (15 February) instead of six months earlier.

For dramatic effect, he makes the Capitol the venue of Caesar's death rather than the Curia Pompeia (Curia of Pompey).

Caesar's murder, the funeral, Antony's oration, the reading of the will and the arrival of Octavius all take place on the same day in the play. However, historically, the assassination took place on 15 March (The Ides of March), the will was published on 18 March, the funeral was on 20 March, and Octavius arrived only in May.

Shakespeare makes the Triumvirs meet in Rome instead of near Bononia to avoid an additional locale.

He combines the two Battles of Philippi although there was a 20-day interval between them.

Shakespeare gives Caesar's last words as "Et tu, Brute? ("And you, Brutus?"). Plutarch and Suetonius each report that he said nothing, with Plutarch adding that he pulled his toga over his head when he saw Brutus among the conspirators, though Suetonius does record other reports that Caesar said in Greek "καὶ σὺ, τέκνον;" (Kai su, teknon?, "And you, child?") The Latin words Et tu, Brute?, however, were not devised by Shakespeare for this play since they are attributed to Caesar in earlier Elizabethan works and had become conventional by 1599.

Shakespeare deviated from these historical facts to curtail time and compress the facts so that the play could be staged more easily. The tragic force is condensed into a few scenes for heightened effect.

DATE AND TEXT

Julius Caesar was originally published in the First Folio of 1623, but a performance was mentioned by Thomas Platter the

Younger in his diary in September 1599. The play is not mentioned in the list of Shakespeare's plays published by Francis Meres in 1598. Based on these two points, as well as a number of contemporary allusions, and the belief that the play is similar to Hamlet in vocabulary, and to Henry V and As You Like It in metre, scholars have suggested 1599 as a probable date.

The text of Julius Caesar in the First Folio is the only authoritative text for the play. The Folio text is notable for its quality and consistency; scholars judge it to have been set into type from a theatrical prompt-book.

The play contains many anachronistic elements from the Elizabethan era. The characters mention objects such as hats and doublets (large, heavy jackets) – neither of which existed in ancient Rome. Caesar is mentioned to be wearing an Elizabethan doublet instead of a Roman toga. At one point a clock is heard to strike and Brutus notes it with "Count the clock".

ANALYSIS AND CRITICISM

Historical background

Maria Wyke has written that the play reflects the general anxiety of Elizabethan England over succession of leadership. At the time of its creation and first performance, Queen Elizabeth, a strong ruler, was elderly and had refused to name a successor, leading to worries that a civil war similar to that of Rome might break out after her death.

Protagonist debate

Critics of Shakespeare's play Julius Caesar differ greatly on their views of Caesar and Brutus. Many have debated whether Caesar or Brutus is the protagonist of the play, because of the title character's death in Act Three, Scene One. But Caesar compares himself to the Northern Star, and perhaps it would be foolish not to consider him as the axial character of the play, around whom the entire story turns. Intertwined in this debate is a smattering of philosophical and psychological ideologies on republicanism and monarchism. One author, Robert C. Reynolds, devotes attention to the names or epithets given to both Brutus and Caesar in his essay "Ironic Epithet in Julius Caesar". This author points out that Casca praises Brutus at face value, but then inadvertently compares him to a disreputable joke of a man by calling him an alchemist, "Oh, he sits high in all the people's hearts,/ And that which would appear offence in us/ His countenance, like richest alchemy,/ Will change to virtue and to worthiness" (I.iii.158-60). Reynolds also talks about Caesar and his "Colossus" epithet, which he points out has its obvious connotations of power and manliness, but also lesser known connotations of an outward glorious front and inward chaos. In that essay, the conclusion as to who is the hero or protagonist is ambiguous because of the conceit-like poetic quality of the epithets for Caesar and Brutus.

Myron Taylor, in his essay "Shakespeare's Julius Caesar and the Irony of History", compares the logic and philosophies of Caesar and Brutus. Caesar is deemed an intuitive philosopher who is always right when he goes with his instinct, for instance when he says he fears Cassius as a threat to him before he is killed, his intuition is correct. Brutus is portrayed as a man similar to Caesar, but whose passions lead him to the wrong reasoning, which he realises in the end when he says in V.v.50–51, "Caesar, now be still:/ I kill'd not thee with half so good a will". This interpretation is flawed by the fact it relies on a very odd reading of "good a will" to mean "incorrect judgements" rather than the more intuitive "good intentions."

Joseph W. Houppert acknowledges that some critics have tried to cast Caesar as the protagonist, but that ultimately Brutus is the driving force in the play and is therefore the tragic hero. Brutus attempts to put the republic over his personal relationship with Caesar and kills him. Brutus makes the political mistakes that bring down the republic that his ancestors created. He acts on his passions, does not gather enough evidence to make reasonable decisions and is manipulated by Cassius and the other conspirators.

Traditional readings of the play may maintain that Cassius and the other conspirators are motivated largely by envy and ambition, whereas Brutus is motivated by the demands of honor and patriotism. Certainly this is the view that Antony expresses in the final scene. But one of the central strengths of the play is that it resists categorising its characters as either simple heroes or villains. The political journalist and classicist Garry Wills maintains that "This play is distinctive because it has no villains".

It is a drama famous for the difficulty of deciding which role to emphasise. The characters rotate around each other like the plates of a Calder mobile. Touch one and it affects the position of all the others. Raise one, another sinks. But they keep coming back into a precarious balance.

Wills' contemporary interpretation leans more toward recognition of the conscious, sub-conscious nature of human actions and interactions. In this, the role of Cassius becomes paramount.

PERFORMANCE HISTORY

The play was likely one of Shakespeare's first to be performed at the Globe Theatre. Thomas Platter the Younger, a Swiss traveller, saw a tragedy about Julius Caesar at a Bankside theatre on 21 September 1599 and this was most likely Shakespeare's play, as there is no obvious alternative candidate. (While the story of Julius Caesar was dramatised repeatedly in the Elizabethan/Jacobean period, none of the other plays known are as good a match with Platter's description as Shakespeare's play.)

After the theatres re-opened at the start of the Restoration era, the play was revived by Thomas Killigrew's King's Company in 1672. Charles Hart initially played Brutus, as did Thomas Betterton in later productions. Julius Caesar was one of the very few Shakespearean plays that was not adapted during the Restoration period or the eighteenth century.

ADAPTATIONS AND CULTURAL

REFERENCES

One of the earliest cultural references to the play came in Shakespeare's own Hamlet. Prince Hamlet asks Polonius about his career as a thespian at university, Polonius replies "I did enact Julius Caesar. I was killed i' th' Capitol. Brutus killed me." This is a likely meta-reference, as Richard Burbage is generally accepted to have played leading men Brutus and Hamlet, and the older John Heminges to have played Caesar and Polonius.

In 1851 the German composer Robert Schumann wrote a concert overture Julius Caesar, inspired by Shakespeare's play. Other musical settings include those by Giovanni Bononcini, Hans von Bülow, Felix Draeseke, Josef Bohuslav Foerster, John Ireland, John Foulds, Gian Francesco Malipiero, Manfred Gurlitt, Darius Milhaud and Mario Castelnuovo-Tedesco.

The Canadian comedy duo Wayne and Shuster parodied Julius Caesar in their 1958 sketch Rinse the Blood off My Toga. Flavius Maximus, Private Roman Eye, is hired by Brutus to investigate the death of Caesar. The police procedural combines Shakespeare, Dragnet, and vaudeville jokes and was first broadcast on The Ed Sullivan Show.

The 1960 film An Honourable Murder is a modern reworking of the play.

In 1973 the BBC made a television play Heil Caesar, written by John Griffith Bowen. This was an adaptation of the play put into a modern setting in an unnamed country, with references to recent events in a few countries. It was intended as an introduction to Shakespeare's play for schoolchildren, but it proved good enough to be shown on adult television, and a stage version was later produced.

In 1984 the Riverside Shakespeare Company of New York City produced a modern dress Julius Caesar set in contemporary Washington, called simply CAESAR!, starring Harold Scott as Brutus, Herman Petras as Caesar, Marya Lowry as Portia, Robert Walsh as Antony, and Michael Cook as Cassius, directed by W. Stuart McDowell at The Shakespeare Center.

In 2006, Chris Taylor from the Australian comedy team The Chaser wrote a comedy musical called Dead Caesar which was shown at the Sydney Theatre Company in Sydney.

The line "The Evil That Men Do", from the speech made by Mark Antony following Caesar's death ("The evil that men do lives after them; The good is oft interred with their bones.") has had many references in media, including the titles of an Iron Maiden song, a politically oriented film directed by J. Lee Thompson in 1984 and a Buffy the Vampire Slayer novel.

Shakespeare's use of this line may have been influenced by the Greek playwright Euripides (c. 480-406 BC), who wrote, "When good men die their goodness does not perish, but lives though they are gone. As for the bad, all that was theirs dies and is buried with them."

The 2009 movie Me and Orson Welles, based on a book of the same name by Robert Kaplow, is a fictional story centred around Orson Welles' famous 1937 production of Julius Caesar at the Mercury Theatre. British actor Christian McKay is cast as Welles, and costars with Zac Efron and Claire Danes.

The 2012 Italian drama film Caesar Must Die (Italian: Cesare deve morire), directed by Paolo and Vittorio Taviani, follows convicts in their rehearsals ahead of a prison performance of Julius Caesar.

In the Ray Bradbury book Fahrenheit 451, some of the character Beatty's last words are "There is no terror, Cassius, in your threats, for I am armed so strong in honesty that they pass me as an idle wind, which I respect not!"

The play's line "the fault, dear Brutus, lies not in our stars, but in ourselves", spoken by Cassius in Act I, scene 2, has entered popular culture. The line gave its name to the J.M. Barrie play Dear Brutus, and also gave its name to the bestselling young adult novel The Fault in Our Stars by John Green and its film adaptation. The same line was quoted in Edward R. Murrow's epilogue of his famous 1954 See It Now documentary broadcast concerning Senator Joseph R. McCarthy. This speech and the line were recreated in the 2005 film Good Night, and Good Luck. It was also quoted by George Clooney's character in the Coen brothers film Intolerable Cruelty.

The line "And therefore think him as a serpent's egg/Which hatch'd, would, as his kind grow mischievous; And kill him in the shell." spoken by Brutus in Act II, scene 1, is referenced to in the Dead Kennedys song, "California Über Alles".

ABOUT THE AUTHOR

William Shakespeare (26 April 1564 (baptised) – 23 April 1616) was an English poet, playwright, and actor, widely regarded as the greatest writer in the English language and the world's pre-eminent dramatist. He is often called England's national poet, and the "Bard of Avon". His extant works, including collaborations, consist of approximately 38 plays 154 sonnets, two long narrative poems, and a few other verses, some of uncertain authorship. His plays have been translated into every major living language and are performed more often than those of any other playwright.

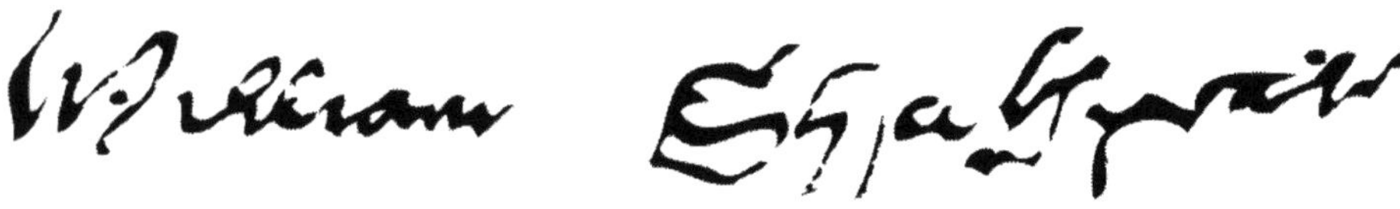

Printed in Great Britain
by Amazon